The Ultimate
FLOWER
ARRANGING
Book

The Ultimate
FLOWER
ARRANGING
Book

JUDY SPOURS

C&B
COLLINS & BROWN

First published in Great Britain in 2001 by
Collins & Brown Limited
London House
Great Eastern Wharf
Parkgate Road
London SW11 4NQ

Distributed in the United States and Canada by Sterling Publishing Co.
387 Park Avenue South, New York, NY 10016, USA

3 5 7 9 8 6 4 2

British Library Cataloguing-in-Publication Data:
A catalogue record for this book is available
from the British Library

ISBN: 1-85585-877-0 (hardback edition)
ISBN: 1-85585-902-5 (paperback edition)

Project editor: Jane Ellis
Edited and designed by Axis Design Editions Limited
Indexer: Lisa Foottit

Colour reproduction by Global Colour, Malaysia
Printed by: Tat Wei Printing & Packaging Co Pty

contents

Introduction

In the 1930s, the indefatigable English floral artist Constance Spry, the first of the twentieth-century's modern and innovative floral designers, wrote the following observations about the qualities and qualifications required by the successful flower arranger:

"An artistic temperament accompanied by dreamy unpractical ways is of little use. Quickness and a sure hand are far more useful, for an eye can be trained more readily than a character changed. An open and unprejudiced mind, a gift for constructive criticism and the ability to see the essential quality in what is beautiful are all valuable assets."

Despite the old-fashioned severity of Spry's tone, her words are encouraging, suggesting that with the right approach and with a willingness to learn how to look and to conquer a few practical skills, any one of us can succeed at the art of flower arranging.

Freedom of design

This book is intended to be both down to earth and inspirational at one and the same time. It describes the practicalities of equipment and basic flower arranging techniques; talks about the colors, shapes, and textures of the natural elements used in floral decorations; and shows methods for arrangements that can be copied exactly or modified to suit other tastes and other blooms. Its aim is not to oversimplify the art, but it does attempt to demystify the process, to free up the reader from any idea that a right or a wrong way of arranging flowers for the home is written in stone.

The book's inspiration is derived largely from its illustrations. We have been lucky enough to pull together the work of a great number of talented contemporary floral designers, and their designs range in style from the formal and traditional to the informal and modern, and from the wildly

colorful to the monochromatic. The book owes a huge debt to their art, imagination, and sound practical skills, and studying their design—how they put together carefully selected elements—is the best visual instruction of all.

From symbol to accessory

Flowers, evergreens, and fruits have always been brought into the home at various times of the year. In general, their significance inside was symbolic or practical: To celebrate the harvest or to ward off evil spirits; for medicinal use, or to disguise the unpleasant smells of early domestic interiors. The myths and sentiments attached especially to wildflowers and plants in most cultures are fascinating, developed as they are from the plants' growing habits, their healing properties, or by chance, from stories that attached to them. As a result, the flowers, foliage, and herbs that found their way inside the home were rarely chosen for their decorative potential alone.

The twentieth century, then, was the first time in the West that flowers were regarded as predominantly decorative materials, without a practical or supernatural purpose. They became accessories for an interior, used to harmonize with or accent decorative room schemes at will. An enormous number of ideas and fashions for flower arrangements have followed, variously favoring the structures, colors, and species of different plants. And those fashions have changed remarkably fast over the years, perhaps because of the concentration of attention on this new and endlessly varied and flexible design tool. It seems that only very recently a fan of stiff, peach colored gladioli in a cut-glass vase was the height of flower arranging sophistication, but now an armful of cow parsley in an old enamel pail is the contemporary ideal. In a few years, no doubt, those gladioli will return—or their latterday cultivars, fashioned by plant experts into colors and shapes that can be described as "new" to give them an up-to-the-minute boost.

BELOW The huge variety of colors, shapes, textures, and perfumes of foliage and flowers suitable for cutting is suggested by the array shown here, which includes fresh and dried garden-grown and florist's specimens.

RIGHT This beautiful
windowsill arrangement
makes the best possible use of
a few individual blooms
snipped from the backyard.
The vases can be added to
when new flowers appear,
and removed when single
flowers are past their prime.

ABOVE Gerbera daisies are here simply displayed in a miniature metal pail. The flower heads are a ragged variety, which gives them added interest.

ABOVE RIGHT In a white painted loft, a white pitcher contains a couple of brilliant pink hyacinth heads—all that is needed to make a spark in a cool contemporary interior.

The joy of all this, though, is that the twenty-first-century flower arranger has complete freedom of design: Older, formal styles are chic and retro while jam jars of wildflowers are distinctively organic and natural; pure whites are modern and minimalist while clashing scarlets and purples are desirably bohemian. In the same way that a whole range of different design ideas for the decoration of rooms is now acceptable, a corresponding wealth of cut-flower designs are there for the choosing.

Although this does not mean that all considerations of color harmony, scale, and positioning of flower arrangements can be thrown to the wind, it does signify an exciting range of decorative options that make the art very appealing. This book demonstrates a considerable number of those options and the ways in which they can be approached and achieved—and we hope that it sows imaginative seeds that will encourage personal variations on the themes to suit your own style and your own home.

LEFT Orange and white gerberas are given the ultimate in natural-textured chic, their stems "planted" into a terracotta pot and tied together with rough twine.

preparations

Introduction

The making of beautiful flower arrangements does not entail any complicated skills or expensive equipment. At its simplest, a few blooms from the garden artlessly grouped in a jar of water can be the most compelling of arrangements. Nevertheless, being aware of the properties and needs of individual cut flowers—how their stems should be cut or whether they will need support in a vase, for example—can make a great difference to their appearance and longevity. They are, after all, living things. There is nothing more disappointing than a beautifully conceived, well-executed design in which the flowers wilt within hours. The mistake may be as simple as positioning the finished arrangement too close to a heating vent. A little basic knowledge about flower preparation can prevent such a disaster.

BELOW *Metal plant containers in a shelved herb garden give a light and airy appearance that would not be possible with the use of more traditional terracotta pots.*

Similarly, it is a good idea to have a few standard materials to hand—wire mesh, florist's oasis, and some of the glass marbles or lozenges that have become so fashionable—and, of course, an excellent pair of scissors. And then there are the all-important vases and bowls and other containers to hold your works of floral art. As large a variety of shapes, sizes, colors, and textures as you can manage to gather together is ideal, providing inspirational opportunities for every flower or occasion.

ABOVE *Flower arranging elements at the ready show the cool, harmonizing effects of green and white flowers and foliage. The warm browns of wood and terracotta anchor the lighter colors.*

LEFT *Colorful purple and yellow spring flowers, collected for a table centerpiece, include the guelder rose (*Viburnum opulus) *which is sought by flower arrangers for its bright, lime-green blooms.*

Selecting flowers

A flower garden can be a riot of apparently clashing colors that would make us shudder if such combinations were used for clothes or interior design. Selecting flowers for arranging can be a wonderful opportunity to be daring and unconventional, in imitation of nature.

Season by season

The sophisticated cultivation of flowers for cutting means that florists often offer blooms from different seasons simultaneously. Stalwart roses, spray carnations, and varieties from the chrysanthemum family seem to be available right through the year. They provide color and pleasure when little else is available, yet these formal flowers in buckets inside the shop are nothing compared to the first spring bunches of daffodils or narcissi stacked modestly in boxes out on the sidewalk. They are fresh, right for the season, and in consequence much more exciting.

Bringing the outside in

The refreshing scents and the bright, pure colors of spring flowers—daffodil yellow, hyacinth blue, tulip red—and their lush, spearlike leaves really do echo the vigorous renewal that we associate with the season. It then seems incongruous to represent quite a different season with flower arrangements inside the home. These displays should positively embrace the welcome changes outside.

spring

summer

Pinkish-mauve cut hyacinths are casually arranged in a simple glass that cleverly echoes their soft color. These blooms have a scent powerful enough to perfume an entire room.

Old-fashioned roses unfurl to display every shade of pink in an informal summer arrangement that is backed with a few sprigs of alchemilla, stachys, and polemonium.

When the year mellows into summer, with softer greens and frailer blooms, flower arrangements can continue the mood inside, using a soft, full-blown peony, for example, with its dreamy appearance and gentle perfume. Traditional roses with their hot-pink, red, and orange petals seem to represent both the heat and the languor of long summer days. Fall brings earthy colors, both of gold and terracotta flowers and of changing foliage, that warm the home as the weather is changing. And winter brings dark contrasts of glossy evergreen and scarlet berries in the drama that we need to give excitement to winter living.

There is always an opportunity for exoticism, in the form of an orchid from the east or a vase of tropical lilies perhaps, especially if you want to defy the seasons and create a completely different atmosphere inside. But working with flowers that are in season means that you will have the best-quality plants and nature herself as the inspiration for your designs. Your home will reflect the garden or natural world outside with a continuity that can be both satisfying and sympathetic.

fall   winter

A glass vase of wild rosehips is a strong statement that color and life are still in evidence as the year develops. Blooms have turned to fruit, with the promise of new seedlings next spring.

Winter festivities are incomplete without a sprig of holly laden with berries. Tucked inside a knotted napkin here, this little holly branch could equally be a boutonniere for a holiday dance.

Shape and texture

RIGHT *A soft arrangement of monkshood, scabious, borage, hydrangea, phlox and myrtle is complemented by the narrow-leaved* Helichrysum italicum *foliage and poppy-seed heads.*

BELOW *A posy, its roundness emphasized by the central rose and a circle of herbs.*

When planning arrangements, the shapes and textures of the flowers and foliage that you choose are as important a consideration as their colors. Some flowers have such dramatic forms that they look best when left alone in either one bloom or a small number of identical ones. A vase of stately irises would not, for example, be enhanced by a background of fluffy cow parsley. Flowers with a less dramatic, even weak, shape which have the advantages of color, perfume, and texture may look good bunched together. Sweet Williams, with their lively, colored petals like so many miniature ballgowns, just don't work if they stand sparsely in a vase. Cram them closely together and the blooms dance prettily.

When a variety of different flowers are used in an arrangement, the choice of shapes and textures needs to be carefully thought through. If too many soft, rounded flowers with elaborate foliage are used together, the effect can be vague and formless. If, however, a few are contrasted with pointed foliage and strongly outlined blooms, the arrangement will achieve much more balance, and the individuality of the flowers can be appreciated.

Containers have their own shapes and textures that have to be balanced against those of the plants. The success or failure of a combination will be affected by the container you choose for it. A round, clear glass bowl has a simplicity of shape and texture that can be used to emphasize a clean, sharp arrangement. On the other hand, the strong lines and coldness of a geometric ceramic vase would suit an angular, dramatic collection of flowers. A vase or bowl should, ideally, complement an arrangement, allowing its full expression.

There are no textbook rules to follow. You may want to create something full and soft in a comfortable living room, or something rigidly angular to draw attention to the clean lines of a modern kitchen. The best combinations can only really be found through trial and error; by putting flowers together and standing back to take in the effect. And they need to be looked at *in situ* so their scale and lines when they are in position can be taken into account.

ABOVE LEFT *Spring jonquils grow in a moss-filled blue and white bowl. Sinuous twigs add form and also stop the long-stemmed flowers from sagging.*

LEFT *Spearlike summer blooms are offset by green and copper beech-tree leaves. The overall shape of a softened triangle gives height on a small occasional table.*

Color and form

ABOVE *Instant color from a few anemones in a jar.* BELOW *Abundant summer blooms, including the ubiquitous alchemilla, are arranged in a lime-green box to provide the perfect color foil.*

Flower arrangements become part of the interior decoration of your home. But they also offer color opportunities way beyond the decorating norm. Although interior styles can be created with easily replaceable details such as pillow covers, you are unable to change them as often as you can flowers. These are the most flexible and instantly renewable of all accessories. One moment flower arrangements can be soft and harmonious, blending tastefully with the colors of the room; the next they can be in stark contrast and enliven the whole mood. And you can use combinations and intensities of color in arrangements that nobody would dare paint onto the walls. Flowers are an opportunity to play with interiors, to experiment without having to count the cost.

Changing the atmosphere

Flowers can instantly set the atmosphere in a room in a way that no other decorative accessory can approach.

The ability of flowers to affect us emotionally is well known and very powerful. Usually, they are cheering in some way, but it is more complicated than that. The effect of drooping heads of pale mauve lilac arranged in a celadon green bowl is worlds away from a flash of red, yellow, and orange nasturtiums in a small Art Deco pitcher—yet each might work well in the same room. It depends how you feel and what use the room is to be put to at a given time. The least romantic of settings can be softened by the gentle shades of garden roses, while a kitchen supper can be given a little modern formality with individual gerberas positioned at each place setting. And, of course, there is nothing to stop you from moving arrangements from room to room according to how you feel and the mood you want to create from day to day.

Flowers are a wonderful way to experiment with and learn about color and its many different tones and contrasts. There are all sorts of combinations just waiting to be discovered. Mother Nature is the supreme colorist, constantly surprising us with good ideas that we would never otherwise countenance, and in flower arranging we get to play her at her own game.

LEFT A serious approach to color and form provides here a dramatic little arrangement of chrysanthemums. The ragged petals are given emphasis by the up-thrust of the foliage, and the yellow is intensified by its totally green setting.

BELOW The gentle effect of green and white alone, reminiscent of a wedding bouquet, is beautifully illustrated here. Fresh and lively green foliage supports the creamy-white roses.

Materials & pots

It is not necessary to spend a fortune

on specialized materials and tools for

successful flower arranging. Nevertheless,

a kitchen drawer with a few essentials and

a kitchen shelf that has a good selection of

various-sized vases and pots will make all

the difference to the finished result.

Fresh flower equipment

The very first piece of equipment you need is a good pair of scissors. Ideally, invest in a pair of floral scissors. They are particularly strong, designed to make a clean cut in the stem of flowers and to deal with tough and woody stems. Second, a good big bucket—preferably galvanized—will not go amiss to keep the water cooler than a plastic equivalent. This will be your flowers' drinking trough, where they will take their fill on arrival from the flowerbed or the florist before being confined to an arrangement with limited water.

The kitchen drawer

Below are pictured the ideal contents of the passionate flower arranger's kitchen drawer. They do not represent a huge outlay, and you can be imaginative about what you buy. A staple gun, for example, is very handy for a whole range of domestic, home-improvement, and crafts applications, so it may be worth getting in any case. Specific ribbon scissors, on the other hand, are a luxury that you may not want to purchase at the outset.

Ribbon scissors

Staple gun

Stem strippers

Plastic flower foam tray

Water-resistant tape

Plastic saucers

Stem tape

Sticky flower fixative

Basket

Twine

String

2in (5cm) mesh chicken wire

Galvanized wire

Spools of wire

Plastic-coated
binding wire

10in (25cm) long
20-gauge stub wires

18in (45cm) long
18-gauge stub wires

Wet flower
foam spheres

Wet flower
foam block

Arranger's support system

On this page are the simple pieces of wire and foam that allow you to work magic
on flowers in an arrangement. They make floppy stems stand upright, support
impossibly heavy flower heads, and generally bring unruly nature into line. For just
the bare necessities, buy some good chicken wire and a nice, workable block of wet
flower foam.

Dried flower equipment

Glue gun

Glue sticks

Spool of wire

Rubber bands

Chicken wire

Silk ribbon

Cord

Florist's wires

Mossing wire

Garden wire

Turntable

ABOVE *A collection of tools, from the mundane, such as rubber bands, to the decorative, like silk ribbon, are worth bringing together before you begin gathering blooms.*

Whereas you can get away with very little specialized equipment for arranging fresh flowers, dried flowers need some serious help. Once dried, flowers are bereft of their natural movement and life, and so successful dried arrangements rely on giving them back some of their original form that they are now deprived of. Although you can put dried flowers upright in a vase, they generally need much more structure, a good support system to get them into shape.

However, a number of the tools of the dried flower trade are ones that you are likely to own already. Garden wire, a kitchen knife, and a collection of rubber bands, for example, are common objects that can be found in most households. If not, they can be easily and inexpensively purchased. Some, such as florist's wire, spool wire, and string are already in your fresh flower arranging drawer.

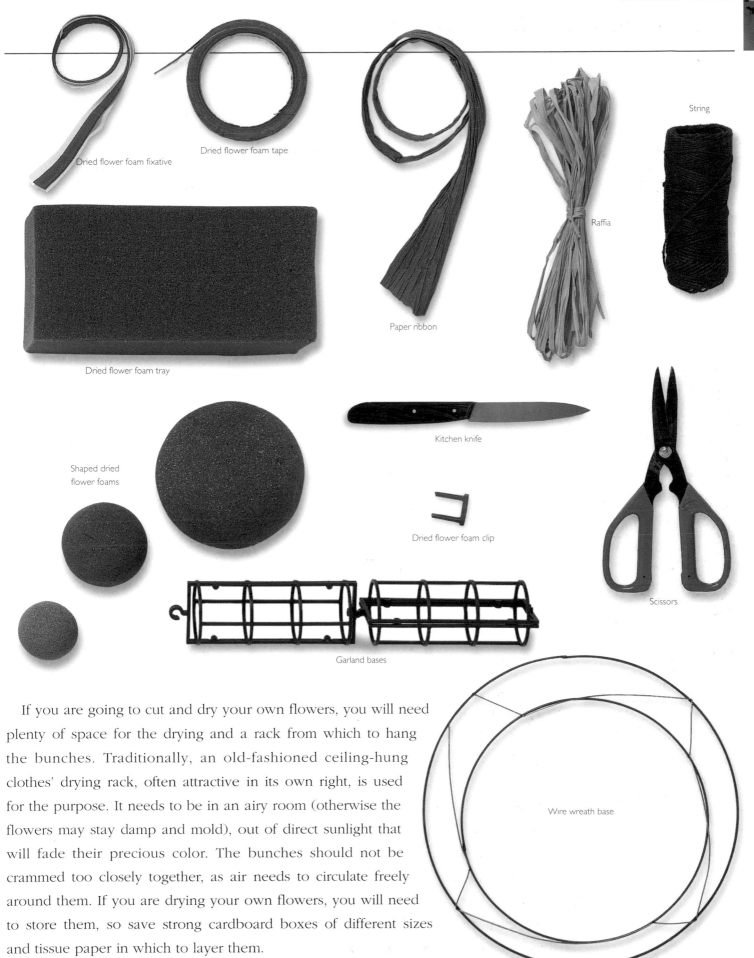

Dried flower foam fixative

Dried flower foam tape

String

Raffia

Paper ribbon

Dried flower foam tray

Shaped dried
flower foams

Kitchen knife

Dried flower foam clip

Scissors

Garland bases

Wire wreath base

If you are going to cut and dry your own flowers, you will need plenty of space for the drying and a rack from which to hang the bunches. Traditionally, an old-fashioned ceiling-hung clothes' drying rack, often attractive in its own right, is used for the purpose. It needs to be in an airy room (otherwise the flowers may stay damp and mold), out of direct sunlight that will fade their precious color. The bunches should not be crammed too closely together, as air needs to circulate freely around them. If you are drying your own flowers, you will need to store them, so save strong cardboard boxes of different sizes and tissue paper in which to layer them.

31

Pots and vases

Nothing beats a really good selection of pots and vases. You are very fortunate if you can amass a collection from which you can always pull the right container for the right arrangement in the right place for the right occasion. It is very satisfying to be able to put favorite flowers in a treasured vase that looks wonderful with the decoration of your room.

We tend to acquire vases and pots over the years. We buy them because we like them and can't resist, we inherit them, and we are often given them as presents. There is rarely, then, any actual planning involved in our collections. Generally, though, we need to have as great a choice as possible of different shapes, sizes, colors, patterns, and textures. Small, rounded vases will suit some flowers and situations, while tall, slim ones will suit others.

ABOVE RIGHT *Glass vases in a variety of shapes and sizes and even colors, and with different neck openings.*
RIGHT *Garden and wildflowers can retain an earthy simplicity if they are arranged in terracotta or earthenware pots and pitchers.*

It is equally important to consider the opening of the vase or pot you choose for your arrangement. If the vase is generous and round and you imagine it containing a big spill of summer flowers, it will need a suitably large opening to accommodate the bunch. If, on the other hand, you are thinking of just one or two stately, long-stemmed blooms on a hall table, the opening has to be small enough to keep the flowers relatively upright or they will splay out at an angle. Of course, some of these problems can be solved with the tools of the trade—such as glass marbles and foam—but a single stem will never look right if it is isolated at too great a distance from the edge of a vase. Above all, a wide selection of different containers is needed on the arranger's shelves.

BELOW RIGHT *These glazed and unglazed earthenware containers are in colors that can be used to tone sympathetically with a wide range of flowers. They are not too bright or domineering.*

BELOW *Patterned china containers need to be carefully matched with their flowers, but are generally suitable for the mix of color and texture of informal arrangements.*

33

Other containers

BELOW *Small pots for small arrangements, perhaps for a table setting. The large wire basket could hold one bowl or a number of smaller ones, each with a different bloom.*

Our grandmothers would never have dreamed of displaying flowers in an old bucket. But today we have a much more imaginative and liberated approach to the subject. We also have plastic, providing us with a whole new range of containers and the ability to line those that would not otherwise be waterproof, such as wicker and wood. Almost anything that will hold water (and not even that for dried flowers) seems now to be called into play by floral artists, interior designers, and magazine stylists for modern flower arrangements.

This is all great fun, and we can experiment with whatever containers can be found around the house. Wine glasses, kitchen cups and mugs, old kitchen tinware, empty drinks bottles, baskets, cereal bowls, tin cans, and children's plastic toys can all be used. Just make sure they don't look silly or inappropriate for the flowers.

ABOVE *An old enamel pail is ideal for wildflowers, while wicker baskets lined with plastic are a pretty way to hold flowers and plants.*

Informal arrangements

These kind of containers are usually suited to informal arrangements. An extravagant centerpiece on a hall table or an arrangement for a living room mantel might cry out for a formal vase or bowl. But Saturday morning breakfast with guests in a modern kitchen can be lovely with a few modest flowers in a glass jar.

BELOW *This selection of wood, wicker, metal, and earthenware would be suitable for flowers in a country setting, or for informal rooms in town, such as the kitchen.*

Techniques

Ever wondered how some people get
flowers to last twice as long in the vase?
Or how they can get flowers with floppy
stems to miraculously stand bolt upright?
Learning a few essential tricks of the
flower arranging trade is not difficult, and
can lift floral designs above the ordinary.

Preparing fresh flowers

Once flowers are gathered from the garden or brought home from the florist, the very first thing they need is a little wash and brush up and a good long drink. First, cut an inch or so at an oblique angle from the bottom of the stem using scissors or a sharp kitchen knife. Remove the foliage that will be below water level in the final arrangement. Submerged leaves rot, introducing bacteria to the flower water, which often produces an unpleasant smell. Place the flowers in a deep bucket of water in a cool place away from sunlight for a few hours or even overnight.

Wash and brush up

When the flowers have drunk deep and are ready to arrange, neaten them up a little first. Remove any dead flower heads carefully with scissors so the cut stem is not visible. Also remove any excess foliage that is not needed in the arrangement. Removing as much foliage as you can will lengthen the cut flowers' life span. A great deal of a plant's moisture is lost through its leaves—a process that continues with cut flowers since they are still alive. After the essential techniques necessary for preparing fresh flowers for arrangements, there are others that will help lengthen the life

Removing dead flower heads

Remove any dead and fading flower heads by clipping them with scissors at the base of their branch stem. If you take just the top bloom, an unsightly stem end will be left. When the old blooms have been removed, new buds have a better opportunity to receive the nourishment they need to open.

Removing damaged petals

Heavy flower heads of many petals, such as roses, open gradually from the center out. As a result, the middle of the flower may look perfect when the outer petals are fading and dying. To remove them, hold the base of the flower head firmly, and pull away dead petals at their point of attachment.

De-thorning

Using scissors to remove thorns from roses or other spiked flowers does not do them any damage. The thorns are awkward to manage in a vase—particularly in a mixed arrangement—because they prevent stems from sliding easily side by side. It is also impossible to push a thorny stem down into florist's foam.

LEFT. *Only nature could put pink and yellow together and produce every tonal shade from gold to palest apricot, salmon to baby pink. These flowers have an incredibly warm color and texture.*

Opening flower buds

Some flower buds are reluctant to open in water on their own, but they can usually be encouraged. Taking great care, you can pull petals of flowers such as irises open using your finger and thumb. Be careful not to pull too hard, because if the petal snaps on such structured flowers, they will be ruined.

Straightening stems

Some flowers are unruly in their habits, but you can persuade them to straighten up before they are arranged. Wrap a whole bunch tightly in newspaper, then place it in an upright pitcher or other container of water. The bunch should fit tightly enough for the newspaper to stay firmly wrapped around it.

Making stems less bulky

Some flowers, such as tulips, have leaves that fold around the stems before opening farther up. This can make the stems very bulky, which may mean that very few will fit in a vase. To remove, carefully strip off any of these lower, unwanted leaves, making sure you do not break the stem in the process.

Preparing fresh flowers

of cut flowers and that will add the finishing touches to designs. Different types of stems benefit from different treatments, such as searing or crushing, rather than cutting, for example.

Flower experts over the years have come up with all sorts of ingenious solutions to flower arranging problems. Some suggest adding a spoonful of cold-water starch to the soaking water of blooms such as tulips and lupines to help strengthen and straighten the stems. For flowers that have

Stripping leaves and trimming stems

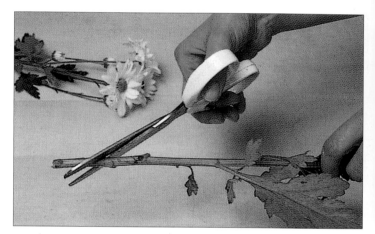

1 Make sure to strip all the lower leaves away from the base of the stem that will be submerged in water; otherwise, they will rot and may cause the water to smell. This is particularly important with flowers such as chrysanthemums.

2 Trim the stems of suitable flowers at a good oblique angle, about an inch from the end. If the flowers have been deprived of water for a long time, you may have to cut away more of the dried-out stem.

Removing airlocks

Flowers deprived of water after cutting may develop an airlock inside the path of the stem, which will prevent water from getting through to the blooms. To remove the airlock is a simple process of plunging the base of the stems first into hot water and then immediately into cold.

Searing stems

Some plants—such as euphorbia and poppies, and even roses and chrysanthemums—produce a milky, saplike substance that can ooze from the stems and can be an irritant on the skin. To prevent this from happening, singe the stem ends with a lighted match and then plunge them into cool water.

an overpowering and not-so-pleasant scent, there are methods of adding antiseptic lotion to the water to take away the intensity of the odor. These days, we can buy cut flower food, generally sold in powder form; many bouquets are sold with a sachet attached. But there are all sorts of traditional methods. These include copper coins and aspirins dropped into the water, as well as sugar-containing alcoholic drinks or lemonade. Although none of them are likely to do any harm, their effectiveness is unproven.

Removing stamens

Lilies are notorious for their bright orange or brown, amply pollenated stamens that stain clothes or the skin if you brush against them. Although it changes the appearance of the flower, the stamens can be carefully snipped off.

Crushing stems

Many flowering shrubs suitable for flower arrangements have woody stems that do not take up water easily. To help them do so, crush the bottom inch or so of the stem with a hammer. This will prolong their life in an arrangement.

Wiring stems

1 Flowers such as gerberas are now very fashionable but their fragile stems have a tendency to droop, spoiling the whole effect of the daisy head in a vase. To provide the necessary support, push florist's wire through the center of the flower head, securing it by hooking it over.

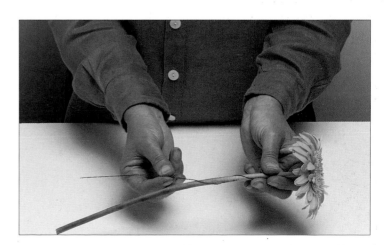

2 Pull the wire through the head gently against the stem and wind it around to give it some support. But do not wind it too tightly; otherwise, you could damage the stem. Gerberas, roses, and other droopy flower stems that have become weak through wilting will hold their heads high if they are treated this way.

Foundations and bases

We are so used to the accessibility of florist's foam that it is hard to imagine how anyone could possibly have managed without it, but it has only been on the market for about fifty years. It now comes already molded in all sorts of shapes and sizes, including spheres. There are two available types—one used dry for dried flower arrangements, the other used wet for fresh flowers.

The plastic foam can easily be cut with a kitchen knife. It needs to be cut slightly smaller than the vase or container it is destined for so more water can be added down the sides as the foam dries out. Submerge the cut foam in water before use until it sinks, a sign that it has absorbed its

Wet plastic foam

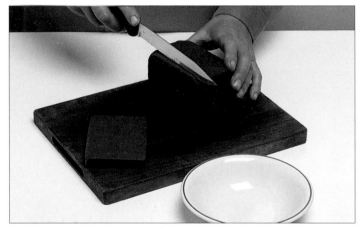

1 Soak the foam until it has taken up the maximum amount of water, then cut it with a sharp knife to fit the container, leaving room to top up the water.

2 Use tape specially designed for use with the foam to secure it to the container, making sure it will be hidden in the final arrangement.

3 Arrange the flowers by simply pushing the stems firmly into the oasis at the angle you want. Think this through so that you don't make unnecessary holes.

maximum capacity of water. When the foam is not in use, it is best to seal it in a plastic bag so it does not dry out completely, because it will then become crumbly and difficult to reactivate.

Chicken wire—easily available from hardware stores—is a cheap and simple foundation for flower arrangements. The most versatile wire mesh to use for flower arranging is 2in (5cm) gauge, a must for the kitchen drawer, which can be used for both small and fairly sturdy stems. Chicken wire can be used hidden in the base of a vase or other container, but more usually it sits in a dome on the top of a bowl as the foundation for posylike, rounded arrangements.

BELOW LEFT A plastic foam sphere, well soaked, has been used to make this globe of white roses.
BELOW A spring flower posy arranged through the wire mesh.

Wire mesh

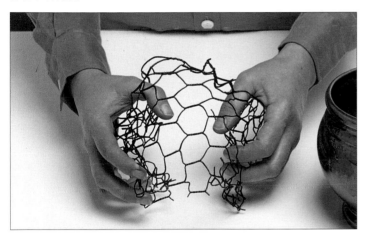

1 Cut away the solid edging of the wire mesh. Crumple it loosely into the shape required for the container. The mesh should not be visible when the flowers are arranged.

2 Wedge the wire mesh into position in the vase or bowl, folding under the raw cut edges. Make sure the mesh is open enough to receive the stems.

Foundations and bases

Marbles and lozenges

Along with scented candles, glass marbles and lozenges were one of the top decorative accessories of the last decade of the last century. They can be used to fill glass bowls in the center of tables, scattered along window ledges, and even be embedded on the sides of mosaic pots. But they really come into their own with flower arranging. Uniquely, they support flower stems pushed among them—even frail ones that you can't force into foam—and they look pretty underwater at the same time.

BELOW *Spray chrysanthemums and eucalyptus are given extra support in a straight glass vase with marbles, which also disguise the rather unsightly stems.*

1 Fill a glass vase to about a third of its height with glass marbles or lozenges. Top up about another third with fresh water, leaving enough room for the flowers.

2 Push the stems of the flowers down between the marbles in position. The marbles will stop them from splaying at an angle across the bottom of the vase.

Both marbles and lozenges can be obtained in clear glass and are almost imperceptible, so they do not detract from an arrangement. They can also be found in a choice of colors that can be mixed together or used alone to create a feature of an arrangement in their own right.

They are able to transform a clear glass vase into a red, green, or blue one, just for a particular flower arrangement. Their round lines can act as the perfect foil to the more geometric lines of stems and some flowers. Furthermore, they are hardwearing and can be used again and again. These simple, easy-to-use objects have a diversity of applications that will provide them with a decorative place in flower arranging for a long time to come.

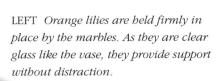

LEFT *Orange lilies are held firmly in place by the marbles. As they are clear glass like the vase, they provide support without distraction.*

Drying and preserving

Dried and preserved flower arrangements require more time spent in preparation, but they pay their dues by sustaining a much longer decorative life than fresh arrangements. They can be enjoyed at times of the year when the garden and the florist have comparatively little choice of fresh flowers. Cutting the flowers at the right moment of their flowering, drying them thoroughly, and storing them correctly are all essential for lively, rather than ragged, dried arrangements.

The most straightforward way of preserving flowers and foliage is by air drying. Although this is in essence a simple process, a few important rules need to be followed. The choice of cut plants for drying is the first step. Many different flowers and foliage plants can be successfully dried, but they must be in peak condition and blemish free, as their imperfections will look much worse once they are dry. Second, if you are growing and picking your own flowers for drying, make sure you pick them at the right stage and in the best possible conditions. Flowers that are just opening are a better choice than those in late full bloom, which are more likely to lose their shape and petals in the drying process. It is best to cut the plants—with stems as long as possible—on a warm, dry day. Picking them after rainfall will mean that they carry a lot of surface moisture that may cause mold during drying.

FAR RIGHT Neatly tied bunches of blue larkspur, nigella, eryngium, linum, white larkspur, and hydrangea heads hang to dry from a bamboo pole.

Natural drying

Very sturdy plants with woody stems can be dried upright in a vase. They need a quarter of an inch or so of water to feed on so they dry out at the correct rate—about ten days.

Drying heavy-headed flowers

Some plant heads are too heavy to dry upside down; they may break away from their stems. Here, allium, artichoke, and large thistles dry upright in a box, supported by wire mesh.

Air drying

1 Strip the lower leaves from the stems of flowers to be bunched for drying and cut the stems level with scissors.

2 Fasten a smallish bunch with a rubber band. This will keep them secure as the stems shrink when drying.

3 Tie the bunch securely with string or raffia, leaving ends long enough to hang them from.

Drying and preserving

Wiring flower heads

1 You may want to mount individual
flower heads, or provide longer,
flexible stems. Here, small flower heads
are cut from the main stem.

2 Place about an inch of wire along the
base of the stem, then wind the length
of wire around to secure it, shaping the
wire stem downward.

3 Cover the wire by tightly winding around florist's tape, which
is green to disguise the wire and resemble a real stem.

Smaller flowers and foliage can be dried tied up in bunches, while larger blooms may need to be dried individually. They should then be hung with the flower heads down, so the sap runs into the blooms as they dry. Left the other way up, the heavier flower heads may become too brittle and snap off. Each bunch needs plenty of space around for the air to circulate, and the drying should be in a cool, dry room, away from direct sunlight that will fade the colors of the flowers. Air drying is particularly successful for small flower heads, foliage, and seed pods with sturdy stems, such as delphinium, larkspur, eucalyptus, golden rod, bachelor's buttons, teasel, barley, wheat, oats, and all grasses.

The plants must be thoroughly dry before they are stored, or the whole object will be defeated and they will deteriorate. The drying time depends on the plant. Grasses that you may have picked when they are already fairly dried out may take only a few days, whereas luscious and heavy blooms will need much longer, probably several weeks. All should feel completely dry to the touch before they are used or stored.

Making a stem

Loose flower heads can be supplied with an entire stem. Push wire through their center, securing with a hook.

Storing dried flowers

1 Use plenty of tissue paper to line a suitable box, then carefully place bunches of the flowers on top, packing them so they lie head to tail.

2 Lightly pack tissue paper over the top of the flowers, to protect the flower heads and to stop the bunches from moving. Cover with the box lid.

Wiring a cone

Cones can be given stems, too. The wire is wound securely around the cone in between the scales, then hooked around the long length.

Drying and preserving

The other way in which to dry flowers is to steep them in an agent that draws out the moisture and absorbs it. The most frequently used type of agent is a silica gel that has been specially designed for the process. It comes in crystals that turn blue when they have absorbed moisture. Silica gel has the appearance of coarse white sand, but it possesses a large number of fine pores that make it much more absorbent than most other materials. It is usually available from pharmacies, as well as specialized suppliers of flower arranging equipment.

Because this method of drying involves burying the flowers and foliage in the crystals, great care needs to be taken to make sure petals and delicate leaves are not bent out of shape or damaged. It is also necessary to make sure the crystals reach into every area of the plant. Silica drying preserves the color and form of delicate flowers better than air drying. Suitable flowers for silica drying include rose, peony, daffodil, narcissus, anemone, geranium, carnation, and lily.

Silica gel drying

1 Line the bottom of an airtight tin with half an inch (1.5cm) of silica gel crystals. Lay the flowers (here, dwarf daffodils) on top, with the blooms up.

2 Scatter more silica gel between the petals so all the crevices between them are filled, taking care not to damage the shape of the flowers at this early stage.

3 Continue to scatter silica gel gently until the flowers and their stems are completely covered.

4 Replace the airtight lid of the tin. Leave in a warm place for two or three days until the flowers have dried.

5 Use a small, soft paint brush to dust out loose crystals from the dried flowers, taking care with the now-brittle blooms.

51

flower power

Introduction

RIGHT *A table setting with a finger bowl is much more glamorous with a few floating heads of* Clematis montana.

BELOW *Delicate flowers that might otherwise droop are given support in an aluminum-covered glass vase.*

With a modest selection of flower arranging materials and tools on hand, an inspiring collection of vases and pots, and a few simple techniques, the creative pleasures of designing with flowers can be fully enjoyed.

This section opens with the greatest indulgence of all—cutting and arranging flowers from your own yard. There is a special pleasure in having flowers inside your home that you have planted, nurtured, and watched grow. They represent a real investment of energy, thought, and care—you can feel a justified pride in displaying them. Garden flower arrangements can effortlessly reflect your own tastes, and they have a naturalness that is hard to imitate with flowers bought from a florist. Wildflowers are even more idiosyncratic, and their delicacy is very attractive, but they should be picked with care and with regard for their continued survival.

The following chapters of this section suggest how you might combine flowers of similar colors and tones: white and green; blue and purple; red and pink; and yellow and orange. The ideas for color-coordinated arrangements are not intended to be limiting (later parts of the book show some startling contrasts and combinations of color), but to give guidelines about harmonious arrangements. Color creates mood, which is obvious if you imagine the difference between a totally white vase of flowers and one of eye-bashing orange and yellow, and it is interesting to consider how flowers in the home work to create atmosphere. Later chapters here also examine arrangements that are largely dependent upon foliage, evergreen plants, and berries to bring the outdoors inside at the least inviting times of the year.

Each chapter has a flower arrangement with instructions for its composition. These can be followed precisely or used as guiding principles for designs of your own imagining. There are indexes of flowering plants within each of the color categories, and inspiring arrangements created by many talented floral artists are illustrated and described throughout.

The cutting garden

Growing your own flowers for cutting and
arranging is worth all the effort required
for their cultivation. A few backyard
nasturtiums or pansies in a little glass jar,
for example, have a naturalness that is hard
to achieve with purchased blooms, and a
few sprigs of lavender or flowering thyme
will give a wonderful perfume.

Flowers from the garden

Traditionally, a sizable garden plot would have had a section reserved for growing flowers purely for cutting for the home. Often, it would be tucked away beyond the vegetable garden—or in among it—and might be dedicated to formal flowers such as dahlias, gladioli, and chrysanthemums. There might also be towers of sweet peas and beds for asters, zinnias, bachelor's buttons and rudbeckias. The herbaceous beds of the flower garden nearer to the house would be purely for outdoor decoration and would not be plundered for flowers for arranging.

Contemporary garden style

Many of us, particularly those living in towns and cities, now have small yards that do not allow the luxury of a specific cutting area and, in any case, we generally favor a less structured approach to garden layout. As a result, flowers for cutting for the home are harvested from all over the yard. A much more creative approach to what is and is not suitable for cutting has also emerged. Herbaceous shrubs and perennials, herbs and trees are all now seen as legitimate hunting grounds for flower arrangers with less formal designs in mind than was formerly acceptable.

It is nevertheless advisable to plan a garden with cutting in mind. It is important to have enough individual plants of one species to allow for cutting without denuding the garden and leaving a colorless gap in a bed. Flower arranging decisions become tortuous if, for example, you want three roses for the dinner table and there are only five remaining blooms in the entire backyard.

RIGHT *Every flower arranger's dream come true: A rich blanket of flowers ready for harvesting. Few of us have such a treasure trove in our garden, but a space set aside for cutting will produce a good supply.*

Index of garden flowers

ABOVE *Scarlet-red roses and brilliant-pink freesias may clash at first sight, but could be the base of a vibrant and daring design.*

W e can only touch upon the hundreds of garden flowers that can be used in flower arrangements. But here is a good collection of common, easy to grow, but potentially stunning plants for cutting and bringing indoors, including examples of foliage and berries. Add your own favorites to the list—and experiment.

It is worth taking a fresh look at plants in the ordinary backyard with an arranger's eye. That pyracantha hedge might be the source of a lovely fall supper table centerpiece, or the eryngium thistle heads that give structure to an herbaceous bed might do the same for a vase of flowers designed for a fireplace.

BELOW Eryngium *sp. is a great structural plant, and its blue-gray color complements almost any brighter flower; marjoram (*Origanum *sp.) has great decorative, as well as culinary potential, with a lovely fragrance;* Agapanthus *sp. is a stately favorite with flower arrangers.*

ABOVE *The pastel hues of scabious and pale-pink spray roses are suitable for gentle summer bowls of flowers, perhaps teamed with contrasting foliage, such as that of geranium and ivy.*

ABOVE *Vibrant fall color from a range of simple garden plants:* Virburnum tinus, *white spray chrysanthemum, hypericum berries, golden rod (*Solidago *sp.), hydrangea; privet (*Ligustrum *sp.), copper-orange spray chrysanthemums, ivy (*Hedera *sp.), and the berries from a pyracantha.*

ABOVE *Sweetly scented snapdragons (*Antirrhinum *sp.) are a favorite from childhood that are now available in a host of colors from dark, almost black, purple, to such soft pinks as are shown here.*

ABOVE *Delicate summer stalwarts: fennel flower (*Nigella sativa*); marigold (*Calendula officinalis*); Lady's mantle (*Alchemilla mollis*); lavender (*Lavendula angustifolia*); and garden pink (*Dianthus *sp.).*

Garden flower arrangements

ABOVE AND BELOW *Alchemilla mollis,*
or lady's mantle, is one of the most
fashionable garden and flower arranging
plants. Its palmate leaves and delicate
stalks laden with yellow-green star-shaped
blooms provide a backdrop to many other
flower colors and shapes.

One of the most attractive recent developments in flower arranging is the use of groups of a number of small containers together. Although each vase or pot looks good on its own, the containers are designed to be positioned together—perhaps on a window ledge or on a small hall or living room table—to make up a whole floral picture. Often, each vase or pot is reserved for one species of flower, so that each can be contained in something of the right height, breadth, and style.

This design idea is perfect for garden flowers whose colors and blooms look beautiful together, but whose stems are of very different lengths. In addition, flowers that have been picked on different days and will wither at different times can be replaced at will; one vase can be emptied and restocked, leaving others intact. There is scope for bucketfuls of abundantly cropping species alongside a single bloom of a less rampant variety to be used to good effect. And the arrangement is infinitely versatile, since the individual parts can be moved around to create different effects. Such designs are necessarily informal, giving the impression of a flower bed brought into the house intact.

LEFT AND BELOW *Garden pinks,*
Dianthus annette, *spread readily and*
flower abundantly in early summer. Just
a few stems in a glass jar are all that is
needed to perfume and enliven a
contemporary kitchen.

Many common garden flowers have a naivety and exuberant brightness that brings instant pleasure. Pure, intense color and simple forms are always fantastically cheering when they are used in flower arrangements. It really is difficult to look at the brilliance of a nasturtium or a poppy or a velvety anemone and not feel better than you did beforehand. They can bring an informal meal table to life, promoting good humor and relaxed conversation. It is no coincidence that ceramic artists of the 1920s and 1930s used many of these bright garden flowers to decorate tablewares, particularly for less formal meals, such as brunch or supper.

Many such flowers are rather transient, blooming only for a couple of days, and are therefore not stocked by florists. This is where the garden as a cutting ground really comes into its own. Even small and frail blooms can be used in tiny vases and jars and in favorite bowls, but you can mass lots of them together to give the most colorful impact. Just one or two bright blooms are enough to decorate a breakfast tray or the corner of a bathtub—perhaps with a few fragrant herb sprigs added. And it doesn't matter if they have a short life, because tomorrow new blooms will have sprung open in the garden.

LEFT *A blue-and-white chinoiserie teapot is brimful of spring flowers—daffodils, polyanthus, and anemones, backed with a frill of maidenhair fern.*

OPPOSITE *Glass jars and old-fashioned milk bottles are the unsophisticated containers for these bright summer garden flowers, their simplicity cleverly complemented by a gingham table runner.*

Garden flower arrangements

ABOVE *Purple lilac is the mainstay of an unusual arrangement that incorporates white tulips, Mexican orange blossom, cow parsley, and cherry blossom. The creamware vase is the perfect complement.*

OPPOSITE *A traditional, but beautiful, early summer display from the garden with delphiniums, peonies, and stocks taking center stage. This tall vase is designed to be positioned on the floor—here in front of a living room window.*

There are other situations where larger, more abundant, and traditional arrangements are needed. You may want a more conservative display in a hallway, a living room, or for a formal dinner, perhaps. Flowers from the early and midsummer garden can create a languid, restful atmosphere and scent the air with their sweet, soft perfumes.

Lilac, which flowers in May and June, denotes the beginning of this summer abundance, and is enormously versatile. It stands well alone, the massed stars of its weighty heads flowing over the edges of vases; and it provides a soft fullness for mixed flower arrangements. Although its stars do drop thick and fast, they can, nevertheless, look nicely extravagant strewn around the bottom of a vase.

Large and more formal mixed flower arrangements need to be designed with shape and texture in mind. The summer cutting garden can provide tall, spearlike blooms and rounded, full-blown flower heads that look wonderful together. Delphiniums, foxgloves, lupines, and larkspur, for example, look good teamed with old-fashioned roses, peonies, and lilies, all within a pastel palette of blues, pinks, whites, and pale yellows. At the other end of the color spectrum, alliums, tobacco plants, dahlias, and cosmos give a brilliant, up-beat whack of color to a room.

The garden copes with every mood and whim—be it for a vase of giant van Gogh sunflowers or a little posy of fragrant herbs. The excitement of wandering out into the backyard in the morning, cutting scissors at the ready, to see where your flower imagination can take you is irresistible.

RIGHT *Pretty lilac blooms are naturally arranged here in unpretentious tinware containers; a perfect arrangement for an outdoor meal or for a conservatory.*

Sweet peas

ABOVE *Nothing but color, form, and perfume in this packed bowl of sweet peas. No other flower or foliage is necessary.*

The scent of sweet peas is one of the most subtle and gentle of all the floral perfumes. It is the perfect evocation of high summer in a temperate climate—soft, a little misty, and understated. Sweet pea colors speak the same language, a happy mix of pale pinks, blues, and mauves with highlights of purple and deep vermillion—but nothing too loud.

These are the flowers of the annual sweet pea, *Lathyrus odoratus*, grown for generations specifically for cutting for the house. It is a climbing plant that grows to between six and ten feet tall (18–30m) and needs support to climb successfully. A simple wigwam of garden stakes, or the

RIGHT *Sweet peas look wonderful arranged just with their own kind, and work particularly well in a bowl that complements their pastel shades.*

ABOVE *The variety* Lathyrus odoratus *'Galaxy Mixed' climbs garden stakes, covering them in multicolored blooms.*

LEFT *Some sweet-pea varieties are plain, one-color specimens, while others have contrasting or graduating shades and even lined and ruffled petal edges.*

fashionable and elegant hazel alternative, will be covered in the long-stemmed blooms from June to September. Sweet peas can give height and color in flower beds, or they can enliven the vegetable patch, reaching alongside their cousins, the edible pea and the scarlet-flowered bean.

Sweet peas seem to look their best without the distraction of added foliage, perhaps because their colors and petal forms are soft enough to need no other relief. This said, sweet peas are a quintessential country garden flower and also look lovely arranged with other country specialities, such as bachelor's buttons and blue and white campanulas.

Designing with wildflowers

Wildflower gardening is increasingly popular, particularly in the form of mixed packs of seeds of annual flowering plants. This is the very best way in which to acquire wildflowers, conscience clear, for cutting and arranging. They can be grown among cultivated flowers or, if space permits, you could plant your own miniature wildflower meadow.

Index of wild plants

As our wildflower meadows decline, we have discovered a new enthusiasm for what we once took for granted and now miss. Where are those bright-blue speedwells and brilliant-scarlet pimpernels that we once trod through without a second thought? Because uncultivated plants generally bear blooms that are less dominant than the cultivated varieties of the same species, a medley of differently colored flowers is perfectly acceptable and won't look over the top. They look lovely, too, with grasses and twigs, in imitation of their natural habitat. Some of the most accessible, from different seasons, are illustrated here.

ABOVE *Cow parsley* (Anthriscus sylvestris) *also rejoices under the more glamorous nicknames Queen Anne's lace and fairy lace, and the more unusual, such as grandpa's pepper and badman's oatmeal.*

LEFT *Cranesbill is the wild geranium, deriving its name from its seed-cases shaped like a bird's beak. Columbine* (Aquilegia vulgaris) *is now scarce as a wild plant, but many species are cultivated for growing in the garden.*

ABOVE *Campion is a widespread roadside and field plant across Europe. This white variety is* Silene fimbriata, *but it also grows wild in a variety of shades of pink.*

RIGHT *Needles, cones, and even bark of the pine tree can add dimension and texture to floral arrangements.*

ABOVE *Lamb's ear* (Stachys byzantina) *originates from Asia, but is naturalized in Europe. The derivation of its nickname is obvious from its woolly leaves. Sage* (Salvia officinalis) *and catnip* (Nepeta nervosa) *both now grow abundantly in the wild.*

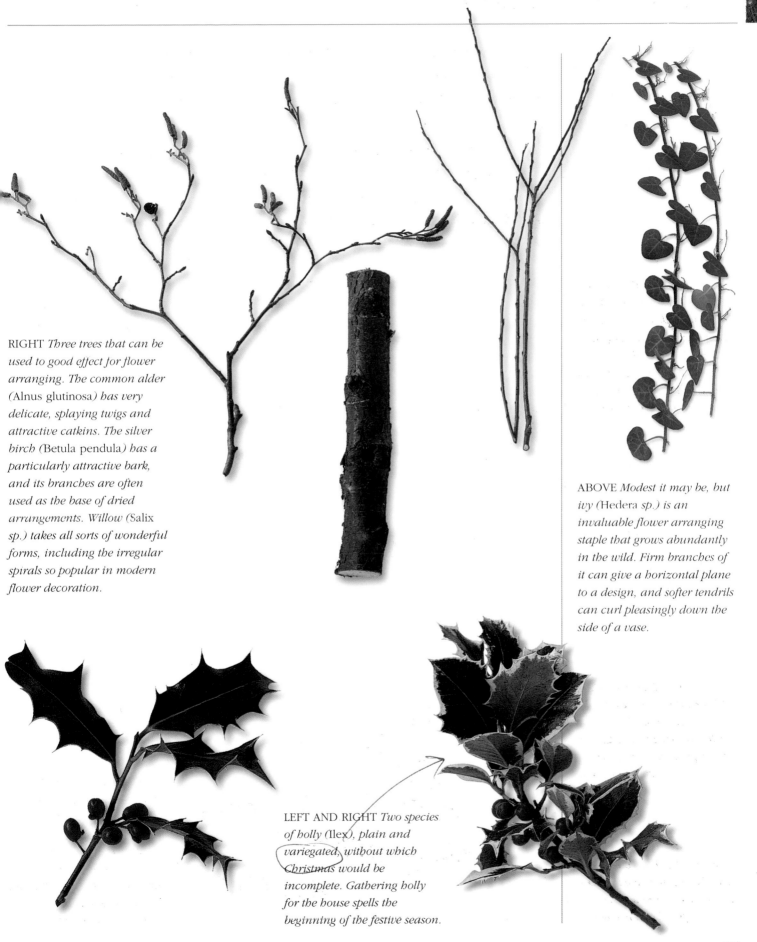

RIGHT *Three trees that can be used to good effect for flower arranging. The common alder (Alnus glutinosa) has very delicate, splaying twigs and attractive catkins. The silver birch (Betula pendula) has a particularly attractive bark, and its branches are often used as the base of dried arrangements. Willow (Salix sp.) takes all sorts of wonderful forms, including the irregular spirals so popular in modern flower decoration.*

ABOVE *Modest it may be, but ivy (Hedera sp.) is an invaluable flower arranging staple that grows abundantly in the wild. Firm branches of it can give a horizontal plane to a design, and softer tendrils can curl pleasingly down the side of a vase.*

LEFT AND RIGHT *Two species of holly (Ilex), plain and variegated, without which Christmas would be incomplete. Gathering holly for the house spells the beginning of the festive season.*

73

Wildflower arrangements

Gone are the days when a walk in the country meant innocently picking armfuls of charming wildflowers on the way. Many species throughout the world are under threat, and as a general rule we should resist picking them at all, leaving them to grow in peace and to reseed at will. But when the highways are lined with frilly brackets of cow parsley and escaped oats, or when we see an entire fallow field of buttercups, it is hard to resist. Pick wildflowers judiciously and sparingly and never, ever, pick an unusual, rare, or non-abundant wild plant. When you do pick a wildflower, never uproot anything at all.

Tastes in interior decoration are much simpler than they were a decade or so ago, with a rejection of much that is contrived and overdone. As a result, there is greater emphasis on natural materials, textures, and the creation of restful environments. The country-

ABOVE *Armfuls of buttercups in a simple, white enamel bucket make a wild, brilliant-yellow display of blooms.*

LEFT *This apple blossom looks as though it has just been gathered in its basket, but in fact the basket is plastic lined and the twigs are arranged in florist's foam.*

side has come to many a town apartment in the form of stone floors, whitewashed walls, and wooden artefacts. Inevitably, a fashion for wildflower arrangements has arrived in its wake.

Cow parsley reborn

Preeminent among the wild flowers favored for such interior style is the unassuming cow parsley (*Anthriscus sylvestris*), a meadow plant that we once ignored as too common and unexciting to warrant our attention. Its modesty now complements the integrity of many a bare brick-walled loft apartment, arranged apparently without calculation in an old tinware pitcher. Cow parsley instantly creates a mood of rural simplicity, but because of its new-found popularity, ironically it now has its own cultivars and can be bought in expensive bunches from a florist's bucket.

Whichever wildflowers you choose, their arrangement should really be as natural and unstructured as possible. These are not formal plants, and to try to make them so would detract from their rampaging beauty—although it is doubtful anyway that we would succeed in getting them to stand to attention. We love these flowers for their simplicity and for their charming imperfections. Containers should therefore follow suit: Use an old glass jar or informal pitcher rather than a precious, highly decorated vase.

ABOVE *Simple rustic charm—this cow parsley looks as though it has self-seeded to grow out of an abandoned teapot, when in fact it has been carefully arranged.*

Mossy windowbox

OPPOSITE AND ABOVE
*Densely arranged blooms
backed by a spray of feathery
grasses naturally recreate a
colorful woodland scene.*

This windowbox arrangement is designed to be done with garden and wildflowers, rather than bought blooms. You could use whatever you have at hand, according to the time of the year, but in principle, try to keep the range of colors that you use to a limit of three, and make sure you have some flowers or foliage or grasses that are tall and spearlike.

The plants used here are: *Senecio greyii*, lamb's ear (*Stachys byzantina*), lady's mantle (*Alchemilla mollis*), *Lysimachia punctata*, foxglove (*Digitalis purpurea*), cranesbill (*Geranium* 'Johnson's blue'), white valerian (*Centranthus alba*), pink campion (*Silene* sp.), margarita daisies (*Chrysanthemum frutescens*), yellow roses (*Rosa* 'Marigold'), variegated ground elder (*Sambucus* sp.), and wild grasses.

1 Spread moss over one side of a long and sturdy cardboard box, binding it in place with wire.

2 Turn the box over and then attach the moss to the remaining three sides, binding it around again with wire, and finishing by twisting the ends together.

3 Trim the moss with scissors. Use the moss to disguise the wire by pulling strands of it across. Place three mugs that are three-quarters full of water inside the box.

Mossy window box

4 Start arranging the plants by providing a background of foliage that tumbles over the sides of the box to provide depth and a foil to the blooms. Here senecio is used.

5 Add height and bulk with other foliage plants, such as lamb's ear and lady's mantle. This provides an informal background for the flowers that echoes their wild nature.

6 Now add the taller flowers to provide height to the arrangement. Here lysimachia and foxgloves are positioned in a fan shape to contrast with the rounder, shorter flowers.

7 The smaller flowers with less dominant blooms are scattered around the box, appearing on all sides for a natural effect. Here, cranesbill and white valerian sprigs are shown.

8 The pink campion is added in small bunches to give blocks of color, and the dainty margaritas are arranged all around the edges to give an informal, pretty, white border.

9 Now the larger blooms are carefully added. Three or four yellow roses create a triangle of bright color. Pink spirea is added to make a background contrast.

10 Any gaps in the arrangement that might spoil the overall shape are filled with stems of variegated ground elder, which gives a naturally loose, fuller effect.

11 The finishing touch, and extra height, are provided by willowy stems of wild grasses, following the fan shape of the foxgloves and lysimachia blooms.

Color spectrums

Whether vibrant and dazzling, or subtle and barely perceptible, the colors of flowers and foliage play with every possible combination and tone. They are an invitation to the flower arranger to do the same, to take inspiration and to enjoy color to the full. Nature's endless range of hues is the only limitation.

Introduction to color

ABOVE *Intense, unadulterated red tulips are packed tightly together to emphasize their startling color in a spring centerpiece.*

Putting colors together successfully and imaginatively is curiously difficult to achieve, as we all discover when choosing clothes and interior decoration schemes. We have to consider tone, contrast, and the mood and appearance that different colors induce, and in many ways the same considerations have to be made when arranging flowers. On the other hand, there is an ease of color with flowers that makes working with them liberating and great fun, free from some of the usual color anxieties.

No matter how many different colors are thrown together, flowers growing in the wild never appear wrong, even when their blooms apparently clash. Even in gardens, combinations of colors are rarely seriously misguided. Some gardeners concentrate on a very limited palette—say, whites only, or perhaps with soft blues added—and their garden designs are harmonious. Others choose plants that flower in a great range of colors—orange with red, pink, and yellow—and still achieve a different sort of harmony in the overall design. Whatever the choice, all is softened by the repeated green of foliage, by every shade of the cool, calm hue that makes the introduction of so many other colors digestible.

This natural color attribute of flowers is very exciting. Suddenly, you can put orange, purple, and yellow together in a vase and the colors look fantastic—which they certainly would not if they were painted together on the wall or matched in your closet. At the other extreme, put white flowers together and there is nothing insipid about them; rather, countless subtleties of tints and shades of white that are exciting in a different way.

The fact that nature makes it hard to go totally wrong is a confidence-inspiring starting point when choosing colors for flower arrangements. We can then move on to consider the setting for the flowers. The colors and style of the room in which they are to be placed are very important, as is the atmosphere that they are designed to conjure up. A limited range of colors of a similar intensity can have a restful effect in a room, while a contrast of light and dark colors is energizing and invigorating. Equally, the colors of flowers may be chosen to blend in with those of the furnishings, or to contrast with them dramatically.

OPPOSITE *Arranging flowers successfully means developing an eye for their colors, which sometimes comes naturally, but in any case develops through trial and error.*

RIGHT *The three-way color scheme used for this arrangement—bright red, bright blue, and a luminous lime green—is the ultimate in elegant modern flower style.*

White *&green*

White and green is one of the freshest of color combinations. It is restful, harmonious, and undemanding. Together, the two colors have a purity of appeal, reminding us of the first snowdrops in winter and of bridal bouquets. There is a corresponding depth in the different textured tones of their many shades.

Index of white and green flowers

Golden feverfew (Tanacetum parthenium 'Aureum') is a completely hardy perennial plant of simple, wild appearance. Its modest charms are perfect for a little table decoration.

The beautiful Madonna lily (Lilium candidum) has been cultivated for an astonishing 3,500 years and is now an indispensable cut flower, grown both commercially and by appreciative gardeners.

The scented jasmine (Jasminum polyanthum) is an easy garden climber to grow. It is a very adaptable flower for arrangements, where it can be cut to stand and support other blooms or to hang down in tendrils.

White flowers have it all—from the naivety of a bunch of garden daisies to the full-blown sophistication of an orchid direct from the East. They provide lightness and visual space in a colorful arrangement; they deal dramatic contrast when teamed with one other color, such as bright blue; or they stand alone with the utmost dignity. Old-fashioned white roses in a bowl look instantly antique, whereas giant white lilies bursting from the top of long stems look supremely modern. Meanwhile, green foliage—and perhaps green flowers—is essential to almost every flower arrangement, providing structure, texture, and a calming color base.

LEFT *A camellia, with its full round bloom, contrasts with the spiky Christmas box (Sarcococca hookeriana).*

RIGHT *This series of white and green flowers and foliage are classics of contemporary arrangements. From left to right: hosta; aster; euphorbia; lisianthus; Easter lily; Cotinus coggygria; campion; and dogwood.*

RIGHT *Two garden stalwarts that offer structure for flower arrangements: Broom (Genista* sp.) *and senecio (Senecio laxifolius).*

This delicately colored orchid (Cymbidium 'Highland Canary') has all the subtle elegance we associate with Eastern style. One single bloom in a tall white ceramic vase is simply stunning.

A few stems of Lilium *'Casa Blanca' fill a room with an intense, heady perfume that has secured the flower's position as one of the most popular blooms for pot plants and arrangements.*

The scented, resilient, waxy flowers of Stephanotis floribunda *make it one of the most popular flowers for a bride's bouquet. It is also increasingly fashionable as a cut flower for the home.*

Elegant and understated

Although technically white is not a color at all, in the flower pantheon it comes in many different shades. Pure-white snowdrops have a brightness that is intensified by the clear, mid-green of their stems and leaves. Old-fashioned white roses have a creaminess that is emphasized by the velvety, non-reflective texture of their petals. And white lilies often have orange or russet-brown stamens that throw their purity of color into dramatic relief. Some whites are almost pink, some nearly yellow, and some verge on green.

Completely green flowers are comparatively rare. The wonderful perennial plant lady's mantle (*Alchemilla mollis*) is an exception, with its flower brackets laden with little lime-green stars. It is a flower arranger's fashionable dream, used to bring out the intensity of other colors, particularly blues and dark reds, and it provides a perfect backdrop for a selection of pure-white flowers in a display.

There is currently a vogue for green blooms as opposed to green foliage. Green flowers tend to come in a wonderful, luminous lime that enhances whatever other color it is teamed with. It looks particularly good with white, with bright mid-blue, and with scarlet. Among the popular green-flowering plants now grown for cutting in gardens and available at florists are the euphorbias, with vivid and delicate bracts of small flowers held on very upright stems, which are perfect for height and background. A number of hellebores also have green flowers that offer the same potential. In addition, there are now cultivars of many flowers that are wholly or partly green, including tulips and tobacco plants.

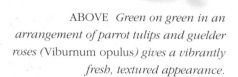

ABOVE *Green on green in an arrangement of parrot tulips and guelder roses* (Viburnum opulus) *gives a vibrantly fresh, textured appearance.*

OPPOSITE *A few tall sprigs of greenish-white contrast perfectly with the blue accessories on the desk and brighten up this office on a landing.*

RIGHT *A medley of pale green and white is heightened by the black centers of tiny blooms, arranged in a small cut-glass vase.*

Elegant and understated

LEFT A large glass vase of Amazon lilies (Eucharis amazonica) complements the neutral colors and hard surfaces of this contemporary room.

Predominantly white flower arrangements may lack the drama of brighter colors, but they are nevertheless striking. They allow the shapes and textures of the blooms and their foliage an importance that is sometimes lost in more colorful designs. In contemporary monochromatic rooms that rely on the structures of the surfaces for decorative effect rather than on a number of introduced colors, white flowers can be absolutely the last word in modern style. They are equally monochromatic, and, similarly, the texture of petals and foliage are often the elements of main interest.

Although at first it might seem easy and straightforward to put a few white blooms in a vase, in fact, the manner in which the flowers are positioned and, particularly, their container become even more crucial to the effect of the whole design. With something so apparently simple, there is very little margin for decorative error. An arrangement of delicate white or green flower flowers will just not look right in brightly colored, patterned, or heavyweight vases or pitchers. The ethereal quality of tall white flowers needs similar qualities in their container.

Glass vases, sparkling and translucent in the manner of many white flowers, are an obvious solution, as demonstrated by the arrangements illustrated here, and those over the page. Glass reflects the flowers and, when clear and filled with water, appears weightless, allowing the elegance of the blooms to shine through. Its colorlessness enhances the intensity of white and green, whereas a colored container would dominate the flowers, making them less formal and less elegant.

OPPOSITE Glasses stuffed with crumpled cellophane provide an icy, glittering base for the stars of white narcissi that flower in very early spring.

BELOW Sculptural white lilies curl confidently out of a small-necked, silvered glass vase, providing a wonderful injection of perfume into the room.

Elegant and understated

BELOW *A goblet vase is extravagantly filled with white and palest pink peonies—these are mature and traditional flowers for a similar style of room.*

While simple white flowers are striking and understated in modern, high-tech rooms, more ebullient and blowsy whites can be used to soften more traditional interiors. For example, elaborate and highly decorated living rooms and dining rooms can begin to look positively chaotic if a couple of vases of brightly colored flowers are introduced into the melee. A room that already has a number of colors used in its decoration, along with patterned upholstery and curtains and many small and highly decorative accessories, needs neutral flower arrangements that will add a sense of space and tranquility to the overall picture.

By the same token, simple single stems or tall white lilies will fight with the decorative style of the room. White and green provide the restful space, but they need to have the same decorative nature. More rounded decorations, with rounded blooms—and perhaps a mass of them—and an abundance of foliage are appropriate for traditional settings. Rooms for relaxation in deep sofas beside the fire call out for relaxed flower arrangements, rather than something demandingly stylish and precise.

Experimenting with white and green is a good starting point for learning about arranging flowers. Using a comparative lack of color makes it easier to concentrate on the other aspects—shape and height, texture and perfume—which are essential to successful designs. With experience in these elements, you have a good basis from which to launch yourself into the dazzling world of flower color.

OPPOSITE *The reflective and highly decorative surfaces of wood, glass, and silver are softened by a vase of tumbling white and green flowers and foliage.*

Mixing early summer whites

There is pretty-pretty and there is proper-pretty, and this lovely arrangement of predominantly white, early-summer garden flowers is of the latter kind. It is irresistible and abundant, but it does not go over the top, and is in fact the skilled and structured work of a floral designer. A small accent of color is given by the pink columbines, cleverly chosen for their pale-yellow trumpets only a shade darker than the creamy whites. The cuboid glass vase is a good contrast to the rounded shape of the design, but it is plain enough to offer no visual competition.

1 Fill a vase three-quarters full with water. Strip the lower leaves from stems of Solomon's seal and lady's mantle, and arrange them diagonally to give a round frame for the other flowers.

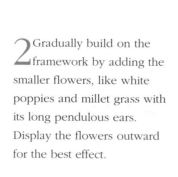

2 Gradually build on the framework by adding the smaller flowers, like white poppies and millet grass with its long pendulous ears. Display the flowers outward for the best effect.

3 Now the showiest flowers can be added to give definition to the design. Insert fully flowering white peonies and strategically placed dashes of color and exotic shape with the columbines.

Blue & purple

From the palest, milky-sky blue, through brilliant-pinkish mauve, to the dark, velvety purple that is almost black—the color palette of blue and purple flowers is extensive. It includes some of the gentlest, moodiest, and most dramatic of all flowering plants, and is perfect for heightening the atmosphere of a room.

Index of blue and purple flowers

ABOVE *The Spanish bluebell* (Hyacinthoides hispanica) *grows well in shady spots and will successfully carpet the ground beneath trees. The bulbs naturalize easily, making it a guilt-free cutting flower in late spring.*

ABOVE *Geraniums are popular, versatile herbaceous perennials, available in an enormous choice of colors and sizes. This pretty purple* Geranium *x* magnificum *flowers profusely, and its shapely leaves can also be used in arrangements.*

We treasure true blue flowers perhaps above all others, for the intensity of their color and for the balance they bring to flowerbeds and flower arrangements that might otherwise be dominated by the hot reds, oranges, and yellows of the spectrum. The person who manages to cultivate the first truly blue rose can be sure to make a fortune from his botanical skills.

Mauve and purple are the link between the blues and reds, the cold and hot colors, graduating through every shade from almost blue to almost pink. They lend drama or a mediating softness to arrangements accordingly.

ABOVE *The most common garden geranium, closest to its wild cousin, is the cranesbill* (Geranium *'Johnson's blue'*). *Towering above it here—and looking very Victorian—is a sprig of pale-mauve lilac* (Syringa *sp.*).

ABOVE *In the middle of the top row is a mauve sweet pea* (Lathyrus odoratus), *and next to it a voluptuous purple anemone; below are the common bluebell* (Hyacinthoides non-scripta) *and purple Dutch irises.*

BELOW AND RIGHT *From left to right here are meadow rue (*Thalictrum *sp.), ornamental onion (*Allium aflatunense*), and* Trachelium caeruleum—*all with rounded, fluffy heads of tiny florets— and a blue hyacinth (*Hyacinthus orientalis*).*

BELOW AND RIGHT *Here are the bell-flowered monkshood (*Aconitum *sp.), common bugle (*Ajuga *sp.), catnip (*Nepeta faassenii*), and a bright-blue delphinium (*Delphinium belladonna *'Blue bees'). In the center of the page is a purple pansy (*Viola x wittrockiana*).*

monkshood

delphinium

ABOVE Clematis *'Jackmanii superba' grows fast and flowers profusely, and can be picked for its trailing tendrils to give shape and delicacy to arrangements. The flower heads will also survive well cut short to float in a bowl of water in oriental style.*

ABOVE *No row of florist's buckets is now complete without the modern favorite* Eustoma grandiflorum. *Its flower heads are held along the length of tall stems, and open in turn. The dead heads can be cut away to let new buds open, giving the plant a long flowering time.*

Moody blues

OPPOSITE *Purple hyacinths and creamy roses packed extravagantly into a blue and white rose-bowl coordinate beautifully with the china and glass on this white table, giving a bright edge to a simple setting.*

BELOW *A tiny pot of grape hyacinths stands alongside others on a window ledge, contrast provided by its own green leaves and by the bright white of the ledge.*

Our perception of the color blue is that it manages to be both restful and lively simultaneously. Most people respond positively to blue, and it is known to be a calming color. Certainly, few are upset by it; it rarely provokes extreme distaste in the way that red or yellow can. As a result, blue is a favorite interior decorating color. Blue and white—and the more dramatic blue and yellow—room schemes are familiar classics, often accessorized with collections of blue and white china.

A blue and white room could become boring and chilly, and the success of such schemes is the clever use of a range of tones of blue, and of patterns, to break up any flatness and coldness. Often, blue and white checked and striped fabrics—such as gingham or ticking—are used for upholstery and curtains to add interest. Flower arrangements in such a room can play the same decorative game.

Blue alone

Blue flowers arranged by themselves have a headiness and intensity that draws the eye to the color. In a blue and white room, flowers of a darker blue than the decorating colors could deepen the overall effect, perhaps positioned strategically against white elements of the room so they are thrown into relief. A blue arrangement in a red or orange room, on the other hand, spells spectacular contrast.

Blue and white

Almost any mix of blue and white flowers is harmonious. Together these shades make a crisp combination with the color contrast providing a depth to any arrangement. Matched with blue and white china, the overall effect is completely complementary. Soft, rounded flower shapes go best with the round forms and sinuous patterns of this chinaware. The blue flowers need to be a shade or so darker than the blue of the china, or they will disappear among the complicated patterns.

Moody blues

The mauves in the middle of the blue/purple spectrum are the color mediators, unassuming flowers that harmonize with many others and create a relaxing, calming mood. Mauve flowers are restful on the eye, particularly when they are toned with gray-green foliage, giving a dusky effect.

All three of the arrangements here feature scabious, a modest wild plant that is now cultivated as a very desirable garden and florist's flower. It occurs naturally in shades from pale lilac to purple, but it is now cultivated in a range of shades, some virtually pinkish red, others white, and even orange. Because the flower heads of scabious are held aloft on very long, slim stems, well away from its scanty foliage, the plant is a very versatile one for floral designers to work with. It adds height to arrangements, fills gaps, and with its subtle shades of lilac it can also provide a visual link—and a rest for the eye—between other colors. And it is not carrying a weight of foliage that might spoil the design.

Scabious has a way of looking instantly antique, and therefore tasteful and valuable, particularly when it is arranged in metal containers. A "modern antique" effect is achieved with angular zinc; country house grandeur with the use of silver, and something almost medieval in feel if scabious is placed in a pewter container. The purple-pink shades of the flowers also look particularly good combined with darker, purple/blue and with soft, mauve-pinks and silvery green foliage. These colors have the softness of midsummer; they are a visual retreat from the heat of the day.

ABOVE *Scabious is used in a voluptuous summer arrangement with monkshood, borage, hydrangea, penstemon, phlox, and myrtle. Gray-green foliage and poppy seedheads keep the tone cool and calm.*

OPPOSITE *Contemporary understatement in an arrangement of scabious in a zinc, studded container on a weathered wooden sill. Mauves and grays merge, lending the design an ethereal appeal.*

LEFT *This design is somewhere between fresh and dried, emphasizing its antique appearance. Scabious is mixed with love-in-a-mist seed pods and copper foliage.*

Moody blues

ABOVE This is a planted trough masquerading as a cut arrangement. It contains purple summer bedding plants—petunias, impatiens, and verbena.

BELOW A fireplace, when not in use, is perfect for a tall, triangular display. Here a mixture of garden delphiniums fills the space with an explosion of blue.

Given that we love blue flowers, we value the bluest of them all—the delphinium—most highly. In a cottage garden, for example, it is the stately spears of intense, bright-blue delphiniums that catch our eye. They are difficult to grow successfully. Slugs love to chew through the base of the stems; and the stems are fragile enough to snap in the wind or heavy rainfall. Stately but vulnerable, in cool blues that are somehow also warm and bright, delphiniums have a strong, ambiguous appeal.

Along with other flowers at this darker end of the blue/purple palette, delphiniums have bright, slightly acidic-green stems and foliage that provide good color contrast to their blooms. The blues are intensified against this green, so often they need no other accompaniment; they work well and dramatically when arranged on their own.

Purple is a mysterious color, one with an inbuilt opulence. The color was highly prized by the Romans, who made it a mark of high social rank. Dark purples absorb light to such an extent that they always appear

velvety, textured, and rich. The color is, of course, a royal one, which is used to impress. It is also a religious one, used to dress churches or temples at the most somber times in their calendars. Purple flowers can be fantastically theatrical, arranged alone and positioned against a white wall, or providing the drama in a toning design of pinks and mauves. Used with a contrasting color, purple flowers look modern, exciting, and original—with scarlet or lime green, for example, or with orange or cerise.

BELOW *A blue and white room, with matching glassware, is given a twist with a vase of wild-looking flowers that push the color range into purples and palest pinks.*

Spring anemone bowl

If colors are matched too precisely—either in interior decoration or with flower designs—the effect may be correct, but it may also be bland. Pushing the color edge in one direction or the other adds excitement. This anemone arrangement takes a blue and white bowl and fills it with purple and cream flowers, echoing the theme of the china. By jarring the idea slightly, it draws the eye into noticing the flowers. Gray-green foliage, which is easy on the eye, then adds a stabilizing influence at just the right level. The flowers themselves are delicate enough in form to complement the chinoiserie painting on the bowl.

1 A blue and white bowl is filled with water and given a wire mesh dome to support the flowers. Sprigs of senecio are cut to about 6in (15cm) in length, their lower foliage removed, and the sprigs arranged around the edge of the bowl.

2 The senecio is then filled in all around, creating a complete covering for the blooms. It follows the domed shape of the wire and also disguises it so none of the wire can be seen.

3 The anemones are stripped of their lower leaves, their stems trimmed so they will stand just a bit higher than the senecio carpet. The flower faces should be turned outward.

4 The anemones are the focus for the display. They are placed evenly all around and all over the arrangement, so it eventually looks equally attractive when viewed from any angle.

5 White comfrey is also trimmed to length, and single stems are added to the arrangement all around, enough to add contrast and to lighten the effect of the richly colored anemones.

6 To add a final touch of delicacy, brunnera flowers are included in little bunches, filling in any gaps and pulling the design into a strong relationship with the bowl that contains it.

Red & pink

Whether in the full-blooded drama of scarlet and magenta or the nurturing calm of soft flesh tones, all red and pink flowers have a warmth of color. Dark red roses are the last word in hot romance, while pale pink carnations have an inimitable gentility. The messages of red and pink arrangements are often emotional and romantic, and always strong.

Index of red and pink flowers

ABOVE *Scarlet geraniums (Pelargonium 'Madame Fournier'), of the type seen in windowboxes across the Mediterranean. They are most often used as pot plants both inside and out, but also survive well when cut.*

Some red flowers are almost orange, and some pink ones are almost salmon in color. The reds and pinks of the flower world merge almost imperceptibly into the orange and yellow palette. At one extreme are hot, flashing tropical reds, and at the other, the lightest skin tones that create a much gentler mood.

Red and pink come with a natural contrast of their opposite color—the green of foliage and stems—which gives them an integral balance that can make them straightforward to use in flower arrangements.

ABOVE *From left to right: An array of the most vivid reds and pinks: Lily (*Lilium *sp.); gerbera; columbine (*Aquilegia *sp.); two roses; marigold (*Calendula officinalis*); a peony, a red rose; stock (*Matthiola *sp.); and glory lily (*Gloriosa superba*).*

RIGHT *A posy of pink and red with a contrast of dark green· Bergenia with its large, glossy leaves, magenta-colored anemone, and sprigs of skimmia with their waxy, dark-green foliage.*

rose

peony

Stock

glory lily

ABOVE *The amaryllis (Hippeastrum) is the most rewarding indoor bulb to grow. It grows at a fantastic speed, bursting into exotic, brilliant blooms.*

ABOVE *Broom (Genista sp.) is more usually yellow, but it now comes in a range of pinks and oranges. The tiny pea-shaped flowers on long fronds can be used as delicate bulk in flower arrangements.*

111

Soft shades

In the flower color spectrum, the softest, most delicate shades of pink and red are found in late spring and in summer—warm colors for a warm season. The flower garden at this time of year is often dominated by toning shades of pink, with countless varieties of rose, pinks and carnations, honeysuckle, clematis, and by the wonderful heavy heads of peonies. Flower arrangements can reflect the heat of the season by using fiery reds, or soften it by using pale pinks. Alternatively, the two can be used to work together in a powerful combination—say, with a bowl of full-blown garden roses in every shade from dark red to apricot.

Peonies

Peonies are an extravagance in a small garden, as the plant's foliage and structure are large, the flower heads few, and their flowering time limited, but they are nevertheless irresistible. When the peonies bloom, they indicate that the year is at last mellowing into summer. Peonies are voluptuous flowers of great beauty, and highly prized in their native Mediterranean. They unfurl layer upon layer of luxurious petals from their dense heads until they stretch out like large daisies. They also have a wonderful, delicate perfume that will gently but unobtrusively scent the air of a summer living room.

Peonies open well in water and should be bought or cut when they are only just breaking from their tightly packed, round buds, so that all the stages of their blooming can be enjoyed. They are lovely on their own, contrasted only by bright- or light-green foliage to intensify the warmth of their pink petals. In a mixed arrangement of summer flowers, the addition of a few peonies can provide the exotic finishing touch to what might otherwise be rather a modest display.

OPPOSITE *Pale pink peonies are arranged with a mass of green-flowering plants and foliage, including euphorbias and ivy with contrasting black berries.*

BELOW *The peony is a classical flower—found wild in Greece—making this stone urn an appropriate container. The peonies' dark-green foliage is used to good effect, with sprays of bright-green lady's mantle.*

Soft shades

Clematis is a popular wall climber, and therefore not the first plant to come to mind as a cut flower opportunity, but in fact it is wonderfully versatile. Many common garden varieties grow at an almost alarming rate—particularly *Clematis montana*—and flower very profusely, so they lose none of their outdoor impact by being clipped from time to time. There are about 250 species of clematis available to grow in the garden, and many of them bear attractive pink, red, and pinkish-purple flowers.

Although a number of species are indigenous to southern Europe—and *Clematis vitalba* grows wild in northern Europe, more commonly known as "Old man's beard" in reference to its fluffy white seedheads—we think of clematis as an exotic oriental flower. Many of the most showy species do come from China, and *Clematis montana* grows wild in the Himalayas. Many flower arrangements in which clematis predominates do have an exotic feel, particularly if the sinuous tendrils are allowed to twine out of an angular container in imitation of how they grow in nature.

Pink clematis can have a softening effect in mixed designs, giving extra shape at the sides of a vase and soft color to balance more dominant blooms. Similarly, dark-red and purplish clematis will give a good backdrop to paler flowers. The heads of the flowers also float happily in a bowl of water—either a large one or, maybe, in individual finger bowls for a table setting—looking like so many little water lilies in a pond.

OPPOSITE *Curling fronds of* Clematis montana *are mixed with foliage plants and green hellebores. The small pitcher containing them is a brilliant choice—its colors echo those of the flowers, and its patterns are perfectly in scale.*

LEFT *A mid-20th-century, boat-shaped ceramic vase is used as a small table decoration, filled with purple-pink clematis. The angular shape of the vase and sinuous form of the clematis give interest to the design.*

Soft shades

ABOVE *To keep the gerberas in this arrangement standing upright, they are tied with green raffia to small stakes that become part of the overall design.*

BELOW *Pink spring abundance is achieved here with crab apple blossom, cherry blossom, and privet as foliage, with dramatic, darker-pink gerberas.*

The many shades of pink flowers provide an opportunity for creating arrangements of subtle gradations of tone or of interesting contrasts. Depending upon the choice of the flowers and their containers, the look can be very different, as the designs illustrated here demonstrate. Putting bright-pink and pale-apricot gerberas together in pastel painted pots is one unusual approach. By working against normal color rules, it is a way of giving the design instant modernity.

The overflowing arrangement below, in its floral-print Victorian vase, is traditional, but it is lifted out of the ordinary by the sharpness of the pink and white gerberas, which prevent the mass of blossom from becoming blowsy and overdone. The arrangement on the right, meanwhile, is a marvelous piece of color blending, in which the shades of brownish-pink hellebores are grounded by copper-colored lettuce leaves.

It is simpler to use a number of shades of pink together than it is to try the same technique with other colors, because the contrast across the spectrum of pink with its green foliage provides a natural backdrop. There can never be a sense that a totally pink flower arrangement lacks color contrast, because the contrast is in-built. This quality can make for some very subtle, warm, but not overpowering-pink and red designs that are interesting, but also easy on the eye.

OPPOSITE *Seen from above here, this design is in a shallow bowl. Dusty pink hellebores open out of a collar of moss and* Lollo rosso *lettuce leaves.*

A pitcher of fiery flowers

Instead of trying to tone down the brightness of the flowers and add contrast, this arrangement goes for the full heat of summer, in a vibrant clash of warm reds, oranges, and pinks. It is a demonstration of how the natural world can put together such colors with abandon and get away with it. It is still a daring design, particularly for a room with yellow walls. The blue and white of the spongeware pitcher adds a touch of coolness, giving enough definition to allow us to see the form of the finished piece, while its traditional shape has a stabilizing influence.

1 The top of the pitcher is covered with a dome of crumpled wire mesh to support the flowers. The shape of this arrangement is all important, given the intensity of the colors.

2 The tallest flowers are put in first, here the orange lilies, cut to about twice the height of the pitcher. They are positioned to splay out from the center to give a full shape to the arrangement.

3 Brilliant red stocks are cut and stripped to the same height as the lilies. They are positioned to produce a tall fan shape—by angling out from the lip and handle of the pitcher.

4 The shorter, fuller flowers are put into position next to fill out the display. An open mid-pink peony is placed at the center as a focal contrast to the other, darker shades. Red and pink roses in full flower are arranged all around in an informal style.

5 Glory lilies and purple columbines add a final touch of slightly darker shades and finer, more angular petals. Splaying out at the sides, they give additional shape and a touch of unruliness to a dramatic design that combines so many vivid shades.

Yellow &orange

The brightest and most cheerful flower colors of the spectrum—yellow and orange—make bold decorative statements. Blooms of lighter-pale primrose and peach create softer and more subtle effects. Whatever the intensity or shade, yellow and orange flowers bring instant gentle warmth and depth to a room.

Index of yellow and orange flowers

From the powerful impact of sunflowers and lilies to the softer persuasions of pansies and euphorbia, yellow flowers often seem to dominate a garden landscape. Without highlights of yellow, a bed can look moody and subdued.

Orange is the link between yellow and red, integrating the brightness of the one with the deep warmth of the other. Lilies, roses, and marigolds provide the most vivid oranges, while carnations, nasturtiums, and, again, roses can be colored palest peach and apricot. Chrysanthemums are wonderful for fall shades—including deep russets the color of berries.

ABOVE *Myrtle euphorbia* (Euphorbia myrsinites*) is one of a huge family of 2,000 species. The flowers of this euphorbia are themselves tiny, but they are surrounded by bracts with a delicate, petal-like appearance.*

ABOVE *Chamomile* (Chamaemelum nobile*) is an unassuming little plant that is usually grown in the herb garden and used to infuse a relaxing tea. Its prominent yellow heads with their skirts of white petals and its fernlike leaves make it a good candidate for an informal arrangement.*

LEFT *This little spray contains the berries of* Fatsia japonica *and the foliage of Mexican orange* (Choisya ternata) *as background to the yellow blooms of* Ranunculus asiaticus *and* Viola x wittrockiana.

LEFT *A yellow variety of the now very popular florist's flower* Alstreomeria sp.
RIGHT *The unobtrusive-yet-decorative flowers of the shrub* Mahonia aquifolium.

BELOW *Counterclockwise from left are a jubilant, daisylike chrysanthemum, a smaller, yellow spray chrysanthemum, and branches of the useful spring-flowering shrub forsythia (Forsythia x intermedia 'Spectabilis').*

ABOVE *Clockwise from the left are sunflower (Helianthus sp.), the ball-shaped flowers of mimosa (Acacia sp.), an orange carnation, a spectacular orange lily, and a dark orange-red florist's rose.*

ABOVE *Canna lilies make wonderfully exotic indoor plants. This variety, 'Wyoming,' has brownish-purple leaves and vivid orange blooms—a combination that would look striking in a contemporary room.*

ABOVE *The gerbera originates from South Africa and is also known as the Transvaal daisy. Its bright, uniformly colored flowers and its simple, graphic shape have made it extremely popular to contrast with minimalist decorative schemes.*

Strong accents

On a gray day, when little natural light finds its way indoors, the colors of an interior can look similarly dull and gray—altogether unwelcoming. The blue tinge of the subdued light seems to remove all the warmth from the surfaces it hits. Bring in a vase of yellow flowers—just a bunch of trumpeting daffodils, perhaps—and the whole mood is lifted. Yellow flowers are instant sunshine.

Sunflowers

Like so many dedicated sun worshippers on a crowded beach, sunflowers in their fields turn their heads up to face the sun and gorge on its heat and light. No other flower represents summer warmth so strongly in our imagination as these huge, naively shaped blooms that look like a child's painting of the sun. There is something irrepressibly spirited about sunflowers; they bring vitality and cheer up any interior space.

Sunflowers are very easy to grow, and you can plant shorter varieties in pots to flower throughout the summer. As cut flowers, they benefit from long, strong stems that can be used for tall and dramatic arrangements to

BELOW A plain, white kitchen is brought alive by a glass vase of sunflowers and lilies. The colors of the flowers echo those seen through the window in the yard, linking the indoor and outdoor spaces.

place on the floor of a contemporary living room, or as a bright welcome on a hall table.

A vase of sunflowers is, of course, fixed most firmly in our mind's eye by van Gogh's series of paintings, in which brushstrokes capture all the vitality, simplicity, and heat of rural southern France in the height of summer. Amongst the most revered and expensive paintings in the world, van Gogh's sunflowers have given these wonderful plants worldwide recognition and popularity.

A sunflower has the strongest possible shape and outline, but there is a wide range of yellow flowers that are less distinct in shape, but whose color can be

Strong accents

used for an equally stunning type of arrangement. The form and texture of a bloom and the shades within it can be as important as the dominant hue. Goldenrod and golden wattle, for example, rely on heavy bracts of tiny flowers to produce clouds of softer yellow. In the color spectrum yellow lies close to green, and an effect that is far removed from the powerful hit of sunflowers or lilies can be achieved with flower arrangements that blur the distinctions between the two colors. Acidic yellows are very near to lime greens, which in turn give way to other shades of green—apple and sage, for example. Arrangements that exploit these colors, perhaps with the addition of cream or white to accent or lighten the design, manage to look both bright and moody at the same time. They bring in all yellow's liveliness without being too dominant in an interior.

Bright yellows, whether in the textured form of velvety roses or spiked chrysanthemums, give a luminous edge to the assorted greens of mixed foliage, setting it off beautifully. Again, this is because green and yellow are close cousins. Other colors would not work the same way: Red used alongside green, for example, sets up immediate contrast; while blue and green is a very cool combination.

ABOVE *The yellow bracts of golden rod are a strong contrast to the purple and white checked pitcher used to contain them. The arrangement has a simple, yet striking, rural charm.*

RIGHT *A variety of foliage plants and white and green flowers are used as a background for the greenish-yellows of euphorbia and goldenrod. The delicate texture of all the flowers gives the arrangement a soft, cloudlike feel.*

BELOW *Bright-yellow roses are allowed to sing out of this pitcher of garden flowers and foliage, which is underscored by the large, palmate leaves of a hosta.*

Strong accents

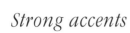

Orange is a color that provokes strong reactions—people tend to declare that they either love or hate it. Perhaps as a result, orange is also a victim of fashion. The 1960s adopted orange as an essential element of psychedelia, but by the 1980s it was seen, unfairly, as a rather vulgar color, certainly not to be paraded in clothes, interior decoration, or the garden. This must have been the pot marigold's worst decade, when it was uprooted with gusto and flung on the compost heap.

Early twenty-first-century taste has "rediscovered" orange, parading it as a new accent color in monochromatic interiors. It is now seen as a suitable color for objects as varied as computer monitors, tableware, cars, and, inevitably, flowers. This isn't entirely good news for the pot marigold, which has been usurped by another daisylike flower—the popular gerbera. It seems that every modern, high-tech restaurant needs a single gerbera in the center of every table to lift the gloom of the matt grays of its interior design. The gerbera is a bit of warmth and a hint of sunshine in a simple form that perfectly complements clean, modern lines.

BELOW *A conventional, carefully structured, triangular-shaped display is a striking mix of yellow and orange, backed by a generous amount of foliage.*

LEFT *A generous glass vase of orange gerberas alludes to the tones of the brickwork and wooden cabinets in this kitchen, highlighting the fact that this is an interior concerned with textures rather than bright colors.*

Yellow tulips

Plain, bright-yellow tulips are synonymous with spring freshness. Cool, mid-green foliage and sunshine yellow aptly capture the energy and promise of the season of growth and renewal. Yet this one flower can be arranged in many ways—on its own and allowed to bend and curl at will, confined and controlled by an angular vase, or mixed with other flowers. The yellow tulip can be encouraged to look full and voluptuous, or it can be regimented into a perfect geometry. These three arrangements, designed by a floral artist, create three very different looks.

RIGHT A square, glass vase contains a bunch of tulips in a triangular shape. The bunch is secured with a rubber band, wrapped with a tulip leaf, which is in turn secured with a knotted stem.

LEFT *A wide-based vase contains a group of tulips that have been cut short so they stand upright and support each other within its neck. As a result, the tulips look natural, as though they are growing in a garden patch.*

RIGHT *A round, glass vase with a restricted neck allows the tulips to curve freely as the days go by. A few stems of lady's mantle are added to give bulk and additional green-yellow background.*

Foliage, evergreens, & berries

At times of the year when few flowers are blooming, the flower arranger need not despair. Nature still has a lot to offer for decorative use. Shiny evergreen leaves, textured twigs, shapely grasses, brightly colored fruits, glossy berries, cones, and other seed pods and containers can create exciting, varied designs for the home throughout fall and winter.

Rich tones

OPPOSITE *The green walls and rich tones of antique, polished-wood furniture are set off by a pitcher of green foliage and red berries in fall. The berries are particularly vibrant against the contrasting wall.*

BELOW *This table setting celebrates the spirit of fall. Colors at this time of year are rich and dark, and when used to decorate interiors they create a warm atmosphere—contrasting with the cold outside.*

Bringing elements of a fall or winter landscape into the home is traditional, with a significance beyond the purely decorative. Harvest is the time when fruits of the field are gathered. Symbolically, decorative fruits are gathered into home or church in acknowledgment and thanks for the success of the crops. We are used to seeing baskets of fruit as accessories, and some modern designs extend the idea—a bowl of shiny red apples and pomegranates becomes a table decoration, or gourds are employed as candle holders.

Since pagan times, all evergreen plants have been seen as symbols of the continuity of nature through the winter months—a sure sign that life has not stopped during the cold season. At the winter solstice, and subsequently at Christmas, life-affirming evergreens, with berries symbolizing fertility and renewal, are brought into the home as talismans.

Rich tones

Recent interior design fashion has retreated from the ornate decorating styles of previous decades. Rather than concentrating on the mixing of color, pattern, and a range of accessories, many contemporary designers are concerned with surface textures, clean lines, and sculptural forms. In some cases, this new austerity seems to be an unsuitable environment for even the simplest flowers.

Fall and winter provide cool greens and uninterrupted forms of foliage or grasses that are much more in keeping with this modern style. At this time of the year, nature echoes modern design's primary concerns with simple textures, forms, and colors. Flowers would be a distraction, and they are less controllable, opening, changing, and dropping petals.

Different moods can be created in a room using foliage plants alone. Tall, spiky heads of thistles create a very different feel to a generous bowl of sagging barley stalks, for example. And a tiny metal box of growing grass, like a miniature geometric lawn, is a different statement to a full arrangement of waxy laurel leaves.

Nor must flower-free arrangements be perfume-free. Fragrant herbs can make lovely foliage designs, and they bring calming aromas with them—of thyme, rosemary, sage, marjoram, and lemon balm. Other plants also have scented leaves. Some geraniums, for example, are highly prized for this feature. There is, then, still plenty of scope for imagination and for personal style without using flowers.

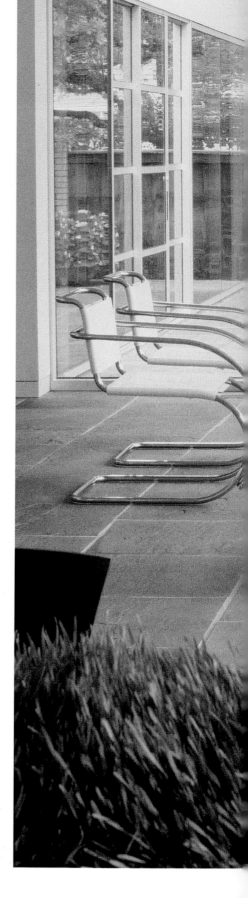

RIGHT *Grass makes a striking contemporary display when grown in wide containers, particularly metal ones. Here its lush and messy appearance makes a pleasing contrast to a minimalist room.*

Index of foliage plants

The diversity of color shades, forms, and textures evident in the plants illustrated here should dispel any myth that designing with foliage alone might be lacking in interest. Green by itself is certainly restful, but its variety here—from pale, tall grasses to luxurious, waxy magnolia leaves—offers all sorts of design options.

These foliage plants are also, of course, suitable for mixed arrangements with flowers, and many of them provide the structure and backdrop to floral designs featured throughout the book. And it should not be forgotten that in fall deciduous leaves change color, providing yet more variations on a foliage theme.

ABOVE *There are about 200 species of* Adiantum, *or maidenhair fern, some of which are hardy enough to grow out of doors and others that are suitable as indoor or conservatory plants in temperate climates.*

ABOVE *A shrubby perennial border plant,* Helichrysum petiolare, *has appealing gray-green foliage. The flowers are insignificant, and the plant is usually grown for its leaves.*

BELOW AND RIGHT *The two plants on the right—*Senecio laxifolius *and* Ballota *sp. have soft, slightly furry leaves that are particularly suitable as a background to rounded flowers. Below are two varieties of mint—*Mentha spicata *'Crispii' and* Mentha suaveolens *'Variegata'—with spiky, ragged leaves that provide interest and perfume.*

RIGHT *Ferns and grasses provide delicacy and height in arrangements. Grasses alone have a multitude of forms, from elegant, bowing, oatlike heads to tall, furry tails and rounder, palmlike leaves.*

ABOVE *Clockwise from above are: Ivy (*Hedera sp.*); Mexican orange (*Choisya ternata*), magnolia (*Magnolia grandiflora*), and rose leaves; ribbon fern (*Pteris cretica*), iris, and hosta leaves; spirea, hosta, and sage (*Salvia officinalis*) leaves. They demonstrate the wide range of foliage.*

ABOVE Adiantum raddianum *is a maidenhair fern with particularly delicate leaves of pale green on tiny, shiny, black stems. This is one of the most popular commercially grown ferns, suitable for indoor use. It looks particularly pretty grown in a hanging basket in a conservatory.*

ABOVE *The thistlelike heads of* Eryngium agavifolium, *and its spiky blue-gray foliage, have made it a very popular plant for modern gardens and interiors. Its almost metallic appearance coordinates well with the stainless steel of kitchens and bathrooms.*

ABOVE *Some more delicate foliage plants: Above are hellebore leaves, maidenhair fern, and* Teucrium fruticans; *and on the right, box (*Buxus sempervirens*), Astrantia, ivy (*Hedera*), and meadow rue (*Thalictrum*).*

139

Structure and texture

A few years ago, the humble grasses found their place in flower arrangements only as a background to wildflowers and as a feature of dried arrangements. Nowadays, growing a lush, green miniature lawn in a wide container, or using exotic grasses as pot plants or as cut designs, are all serious modernist statements. This fashion follows hot on the heels of the use of grasses by many contemporary landscape designers, who have used their sculptural forms to create whole gardens, as well as cut sod to make fine patterns in new, formal exterior spaces. The market has responded to the times, and a number of indoor grasses and bamboos are now available to the consumer. Among these look out for papyrus grass. It is structured like an exotic bush and can be given a haircut to produce graphic topiary shapes in simple vases. Dracaenas are tropical woody-

BELOW *The fine silver decoration on this simple glass tumbler enhances the silvery-gray color and the spiked shape of these few sprigs of eryngium.*

stemmed plants topped with slender palm-like leaves, often striped dark green and white, that make sculptural indoor features. Miniature house bamboos look very stylish grown in metal containers, and several small plants can be lined up to create a geometric effect.

Spiky plants

There is nothing soft or undulating about the foliage of thistles and similarly spiky plants. Rigid, pointed, and dangerous looking, they make a dramatic and uncompromising impression when they are arranged on their own. They have become a sort of modern substitute for cacti, presenting a similarly exotic and touch-me-not appearance.

The most popular plant of this nature is eryngium, or sea holly, which is now widely grown for cutting and can be readily bought from a florist. It is versatile in mixed arrangements, but it is often used alone, showing off its subtle foliage colors that range from metallic gray to soft, dark blue, as well as its striking, angular foliage. Other popular plants of this type include globe thistles—which also make a fine addition to dried flower arrangements—the common teasel, and any variety of wild thistle.

ABOVE *Contemporary table-setting style, in which little pots of growing grass and foliage plants are the only hint of color among silver, black, and white.*

ABOVE *A spiky little metal pot of thistles is an understated centerpiece for an outdoor meal on a weathered old wooden table.*

LEFT *Old garden pails are planted with house bamboos. Here, a low-growing variety has been used to create shaggy rounded heads of pale-green color.*

141

LEFT *A row of different foliage plants in a country kitchen is pulled together visually by the use of identical pots to contain each one. The greens contrast well with the red of the painted plates and pitchers behind.*

Fluid foliage

Traditional foliage plants still have an important role to play in arrangements. Many, such as ferns, are rightly valued for their delicate fronds and fresh, green coloring. Maidenhair and asparagus ferns, widely grown as pot plants, have lovely, soft forms that can be used decoratively to break up the hard surface lines of a kitchen or bathroom.

Foliage can be given a contemporary spin by changing traditional terracotta or ceramic containers for more modern metal or wood. Alternatively, more than one plant at a time can be used to produce a small geometry in an empty space. Many of the old favorites are back in fashion. The lovely texture of gray-green eucalyptus leaves and the pretty plain or variegated leaves of ivies—either with or without their shiny, black berries—are popular again. The deep-green leaves of hornbeam that turn a dramatic yellow in fall, or the lovely green or copper leaves of beech trees that change to stunning bronze and gold tints, provide a range of foliage colors.

LEFT *Lilac, pale green, and gold is a very fashionable interior decorating palette, and the gray tones of the colors call out for something similar from nature. An interestingly shaped glass vase—that echoes the round mirror—is filled with a few sprigs of eucalyptus.*

Posy of fragrant green herbs

The herbs in this posy are chosen for their different shapes and colors of foliage and for the combination of their aromas. All the herbs are edible, so the posy would make a nice gift for a cook, who could snip from the arrangement in a jar in the kitchen. Otherwise, she might choose to hang it up to dry for winter use.

1 A good long branch of rosemary is neatened up by removing the lower leaves. This creates a stem so it can be incorporated with other herbs in the posy.

2 A bunch of parsley is attached to the rosemary branch with garden twine—string will work just as well. The full leaves of the parsley add depth to the arrangement.

3 Stems of bay leaves, sage, and bunches of chives are bound into the posy in the same way, arranged at angles so all can be clearly seen in the final bunch.

Fruits of the forest

Flowers may be extravagant, exotic, striking, but nothing quite beats the juicy fruits of fall for voluptuousness. Berries that were once grown and collected as food alone are now plundered for decorative arrangements of blackberries and even tomatoes.

Many wild plants, modestly dressed at other times of the year, come into their full glory in fall and winter. Preeminent among them, and with the strongest associations, are holly, ivy, and mistletoe. In pre-Christian times, holly with berries was brought into the house in midwinter as a fertility symbol and as a defense against witchcraft. The custom was subsequently adapted to Christian symbolism, so the spiny leaves represented a crown of thorns and the dark-red berries symbolized Christ's blood.

Ivy has ancient associations with alcohol—in classical times an infusion made from it was thought to be a hangover cure. Now it is the appropriate accompaniment to holly in the Christmas carol. The two plants are used together decoratively, although ivy also plays a substantial role in flower arrangements throughout the year. Its black berries are solemn and stylish, and look marvellous with red.

Mysterious mistletoe

White-berried mistletoe is the magical plant of the trio, the one credited by ancient herbalists with extraordinary curative powers, capable of alleviating everything from epilepsy to tumors. The druids regarded the plant as nothing less than sacred. Its berries are translucent, giving it an ethereal appearance that mixes well with the reds and greens of winter decorations.

RIGHT *The fruitfulness of fall is captured on a kitchen windowsill with an overflowing pitcher of berries and hips, and by ripening tomatoes and filberts.*

Index of evergreens and berries

ABOVE *Box* (Buxus sempervirens) *is a slow-growing, hardy evergreen ideal for hedging and, in its dwarf form, for growing in modern containers.*

ABOVE Helichrysum petiolare *is grown for its silvery-gray foliage, which provides a soft background to summer flower arrangements.*

Once flowers have disappeared from the garden, color that might be exploited for arrangements may be found in the berries of shrubs or of hedging plants such as pyracantha. A rose garden that is allowed to progress to hips provides lovely, shapely, scarlet fruits for picking that can take the place of brightly colored blooms. Here are a few possibilities for fall and winter decorations, including branches carrying another sort of fruit—cones. These examples offer a range of inspiring textures, forms, and shades that are excitingly different from the more conventionally attractive spring and summer flowers

LEFT AND BELOW *Holly and ivy as we see them at Christmas. Here the red-berried holly is variegated, and the ivy has been chosen for its ripening black berries.*

RIGHT *Ivy* (Hedera *sp.*)*is such a common plant that its potential can be overlooked. It survives for a long time out of water, and its long tendrils can be wound around a banister at Christmas. Its leaves and sinuous habit are useful throughout the year in mixed arrangements.*

BELOW *The cones of the larch tree are conveniently arranged closely together along the stems, making it ideal for winter designs.*

ABOVE *Usually collected for culinary use as a flavoring for gin, sloe berries have a wonderful dusty, black appearance that can help to create a strikingly modern, dramatic arrangement.*

RIGHT *Scarlet and yellow berries from pyracantha shrubs, other varieties of which produce bright-orange berries*

ABOVE *Chili peppers (Capiscum annum) ripening from green, through yellow, to orange, are borne along the length of fall stems. They provide powerful color impact.*

149

Arrangements for fall and winter

Mixing fruit and flowers together can produce some of the most vibrant designs in luscious combinations of red, orange, and yellow. Here are three different variations on this theme.

The hydrangea heads appear to be merely stacked on a cake stand along with apples, cherries, and pomegranates, but of course they would soon wilt without water. They are, in fact, pushed down into wet florist's foam, and the fruits arranged to fill the gaps and hide the foam from view.

In the center design, one of a collection of colorful gourds has been gouged out for use as a vase. The base of the gourd is cut flat so it stands firm, and its pale yellow works beautifully with physalis (orange lanterns) and fat garden rosehips. The glass fruit bowl on the right is scattered with a few sprigs of clematis—not as a lasting arrangement, but as a decorative idea for the final dish of a dinner party.

BELOW *One reason for the success of this design is that the flowers and foliage of the hydrangeas are variegated reds and greens—characteristic also of the skins of the apples and pomegranates.*

LEFT *The yellow of the gourd is pale and soft enough to enhance, but not compete with, the reds and oranges of the rose hips and delicate lanterns.*

BELOW *Although clematis has been used here to decorate the fruit bowl, any number of colorful or scented flowers would work well. Bright-yellow and orange nasturtiums would look great, appropriate also because they are edible and sometimes included in salads.*

Some floral artists have developed this idea to correspond to contemporary interior textures and colors, concentrating on the acidic tones that are now fashionable for paints and furniture. Lemons are used with chic, acidic-green lady's mantle and yellow gerberas, for example, and limes are combined with the new chrysanthemums of similar hue. Imagination could create many interesting designs on this theme. Cherries and dark red dahlias—or starfruits with the star-shaped flowers of agapanthus—could even be used as table centerpieces.

Blackberries

These two designs give a whole new meaning to an old-fashioned fall afternoon spent picking blackberries. Never mind using them in the other half of the apple pie, cut whole sprigs as room accessories! The fact is that the berries look gorgeous—in a range of hues from pale, unripe green, through darkening pinks, to full blacks.

An arrangement that literally ripens before your eyes is extremely welcoming. And the opportunity to eat the fruit, rather than deadhead the flowers, is a particularly pleasing prospect. Both designs here use very simple containers—one a plain, white pitcher, the other a wooden bowl—that suit the wildness of the berries.

ABOVE *The effect of this supremely fruitful wooden bowl of blackberries is almost overwhelming. The choice of wood for the container is in keeping with the shrubby, wild nature of the plant.*

LEFT *These blackberry branches have been chosen with a good amount of foliage attached so that the large leaves break up the effect of the small berries.*

Exotic Christmas wreath

Foreign fruits have always been a feature of Christmas, traditionally in the form of dried figs and dates. Now that a great range of exotic fruits is available in supermarkets throughout the year, Christmas options have grown. This interesting new produce can be used for inspirational, even unique arrangements. Kumquats, eaten whole, skin and all, are certainly delicious, but they are also very decorative. Their golden skin has a spongy texture that contrasts well with the spiky evergreens. They are exploited here to make a fresh, highly unusual Christmas wreath.

1 Evergreens are cut to about 6in (15cm) in length, gathered into small bunches, and then secured together with florist's wire or string. A selection of ivy, cypress, and juniper is shown here, but any other variation of foliage can be used.

2 A wreath frame is entirely covered with moss that is bound on with twine. The bunches of evergreens are bound on one by one, each covering the stems of the one before. Continue this process until the whole ring is complete and the frame is not visible.

3 A length of pliable wire is pushed gently through the breadth of each kumquat. This is continued until a complete circle of the fruit is threaded like a giant necklace that will fit neatly inside the wreath of evergreen foliage. This will form the center of the wreath.

4 Once enough kumquats are in place on the ring, twist the ends of the wire together. The wire ends are used to attach the ring inside the evergreen wreath, and more wire is used at intervals around the outside to fasten the ring securely.

Living with flowers

Introduction

OPPOSITE *Spring color is provided in a white and cream kitchen by complementary white tulips and contrasting pink hyacinths. The two work together because the pitcher chosen for the tulips is decorated with pink flowers that link it to the hyacinths.*

Flowers can decorate every room of the home, from kitchen to bathroom, dining room to hallway, study to bedroom. The nature of the room, and the position of an arrangement in it, is the first consideration when choosing the colors, textures, and scale of the flowers. Obviously, the tall stems of, say, delphiniums or sunflowers that might fill an empty living-room fireplace would not be suitable for the small bedside table of a guest bedroom; nor would a vase of orange marigolds particularly enhance a red dining room. Yet beyond such evident restrictions, there are subtleties of color and form that can make the difference between a merely pretty arrangement and one that sets a whole mood.

Room by room

This section of the book looks at flower arranging in the broader context of the home and examines how flowers can enhance the activities of daily life and of special events. It discusses how to select flowers that are sympathetic to the environment and that fit in with the interior decoration of a specific room. The chapters focus on various rooms and spaces in the home; on using flowers for spectacular effect when entertaining and decorating dining tables; on incorporating plants into candlelight decorations; and on finding the best combinations for different situations and occasions.

There is also a special chapter that concentrates on using potted plants around the home, another that looks specifically at decorating with spring bulbs, and a third that shows the wonderful decorative diversity of roses. The following pages explore the pleasure of living with flowers. They show that —whether simple or grand— flowers and plants bring life into the home, a feat that no other decorative accessory can accomplish.

BELOW *A wicker breakfast-in-bed tray is brought to life by a tiny vase of creamy tulip heads, chosen to tie the whites of the ceramics with the natural tones of the wicker and bamboo tray.*

Around the home

Color, perfume, and the texture of petals and foliage can be used in displays in the foyer and carry on right through the home, making the transition from outdoors to the inside natural and easy. There is no room that is not brought to life with flowers, and a home that is decorated in such a way is a pleasure to live in.

Living spaces

The first rooms that come to mind when you are thinking about flowers for the home are the most public ones, those used by the whole family and by guests. If you have just one opportunity for a flower arrangement in the home, it is likely to find its way into a living room—where it can be appreciated by many—rather than into a private area such as a bedroom or study. Flowers and plants are, in fact, such staples of the modern interior that without them living rooms can seem quite dead and uninviting—certainly missing something. They have become essential accessories, every bit as necessary as pillows, pictures, lighting, and ornaments to the overall decorative scheme of a finished room. As flower arrangements can thus be seen as elements of the interior design of your home, so they should be given the same consideration. Make sure that their proportions, colors, and styles all work

RIGHT *The pot of gerberas is in full sun, framed by the curtains of an attic window to place the flowers at center stage—appropriate for an arrangement that is so important to the look of the entire room.*

with the room that they are intended for, and that they contribute to the mood. A vase of flowers cannot be admired in isolation, but must look good in the wider context of the decorations of the room and the position in which it is placed.

Traditional and modern

The traditional living room pictured below, with its subdued colors and formal, conventional furniture, almost seems to have been designed around the idea of vases of flowers as finishing touches to the scheme. A small table next to the window, and adjacent to the backyard, is the perfect place for an arrangement to link outside and inside through foliage and flowers. Almost any color flowers could be used in this neutral situation, depending upon the desired effect.

BELOW *Peachy-orange florist's roses add a gentle touch of color in this neutral living room, simply displayed in a glass vase that reflects the light pouring in from the windows to great effect.*

Living spaces

The little sitting area (pictured on page 162), however, uses its flowers in quite a different way. The crisp, contemporary, yellow and white stripes and checks of the curtains and upholstery are repeated in a plant pot that contains red and yellow gerberas. The flowers are pivotal to the scheme, and the whole arrangement is very carefully thought through. Daisies are the floral equivalent of the stripes and checks—they have simple, geometric, and uncomplicated forms—and are perfectly in keeping with them. The yellow gerberas are exactly the same shade as the textile furnishings, and the red ones introduce a strong accent color essential to the decoration of the area—without it the room might appear too bland. The pot plant is, in addition, virtually the only accessory in the room, enhancing its decorative status yet further. There is certainly no sense here that the plant could be replaced with another at random; a different design and a different flower would change the effect entirely.

Minimal contemporary interiors, as we have seen, are even more exacting in their flower or foliage requirements. Where there is very little color or visual interruption from expanses of textured walls, floors, and huge windows, the introduction of flowers can create a focal point, making the arrangement's design crucial. This can be the opportunity for high floral drama and impact that would not be possible in a more traditional room where the flowers are only one accessory among many others.

With a little care in the choice of flowers and their containers, arrangements can work extremely well in less sophisticated interiors to coordinate or contrast

RIGHT *Three small arrangements chime with the repeating themes in this open dining area. They also serve to soften the overall look—without them, the strong lines and the subdued color scheme could leave the area feeling cold and unwelcoming.*

Living spaces

ABOVE *Pot plants don't have to be single-species exhibits. Here a number of foliage and flowering plants are grouped together to give a balance of color and form.*

with the colors and patterns used in the decorations. The bowl of plants top left here, for example, is perfect for its surroundings: The blue and white spongeware bowl echoes the wallpaper colors, while the sinuous foliage repeats the lines of the wallpaper pattern. The purple and mauve African violets nudge the blue color palette along a little to add greater interest, yet the whole is natural and apparently effortless.

The vase on the turquoise coffee table on the right, meanwhile, is an exercise in highlighting and contrasting colors, picking out the reds and darker blues of the sofa pillows, and giving the whole an exciting edge with the introduction of acidic-green chrysanthemums. The green also echoes the colors of the garden outside, and so helps to bring a sense of the outdoors into the room. This simple optical trick serves to freshen the atmosphere of the whole room.

RIGHT *A blue glass filled with blue-purple anemones would provide a powerful color accent in a room that needs a bit of added mood, excitement, and color variation.*

RIGHT *A fabulous contrast is achieved here, with the bright colors of flowers, foliage, and berries. The arrangement strikes a cheerful and fresh note that is totally in keeping with the style of this modern, unpretentious garden room.*

Living spaces

RIGHT *A large, bright hallway in a family home is adopted as a space for living and playing, and the large vase of flowers on the table is suitably bright and lively.*

Kitchen/dining rooms

In many homes, kitchen and dining room are now one and the same area rather than two distinct rooms. There are a number of reasons for this change in living habits. First, many modern homes have comparatively little space to manipulate, and we prefer to use large, light areas rather than divide the space up into small rooms. Second, contemporary kitchens are sleekly designed, no longer quite so unattractive and labor intensive. Most important, we now have a much less formal approach to eating and entertaining, one that reflects a general social change.

Not that kitchen/dining rooms are haphazard; even their informality is carefully designed. Flower arrangements follow suit, and have taken on a natural style that is in many ways highly contrived. The kitchen table may be adorned with a few wild-flowers in a glass jar, for example, but the blooms are still carefully chosen, and the jar saved, scrubbed clean, and added to the collection of vases.

RIGHT *Yellow is used as an accent color in a room of aquatic blues and greens. The color scheme is highlighted with a metal pitcher of daffodils for a lunch party.*

OPPOSITE *The fresh simplicity of a blue and white gingham tablecloth continues in a jar of flowers and berries from the backyard.*

Kitchen/dining rooms

Bright color

Some homes boast serious stainless-steel cooks' kitchens, while other kitchens are designed as family rooms, with wooden floors, painted cabinets and furniture, and colorful ceramics for display and as tableware. The look in the cook's kitchen is usually fairly minimal, with clean lines and restrained colors. Flowers for these kitchens need either to continue the minimal look, or to contrast strongly with it. Anything in between risks looking lost and simply messy. The look in the family kitchen is warm and lively, and a little chaotic. Arrangements of flowers in mixed colors, overflowing and abundant, suit the style. Garden or wildflowers or simple florist's blooms in earthenware pots or clear glass vases fit well. In this situation, a stiff and formal flower arrangement in a sophisticated container would look out of place.

One of the reasons why such informal flower arrangements do need to be carefully thought through is that they can have many different uses and positions in a kitchen and dining area. For example, pot plants may be displayed along a window ledge, a pail of garden blooms on a hutch, a slender vase on a breakfast bar, and a low bowl of flowers as a centerpiece on a dining table. If the number of arrangements is unlimited and the colors and styles conflict, the whole decorative effect can become messy. A feeling of casual abundance is, in fact, very difficult to design successfully without overdoing it.

RIGHT *An arrangement of branching blooms in vibrant and opposing colors, red, green, and orange, gives this restrained kitchen color scheme a boost— and also introduces a bit of character.*

Kitchen/dining rooms

ABOVE *A trailing, ivy-leaved geranium decorates a kitchen windowsill—a plant that grows equally well outside and thus links the house with the yard.*
BELOW *Summer garden abundance, ideal for informal flower arrangements, in the form of nigella, lupine, rose, lady's mantle, and other colorful blooms.*

When designing arrangements for the kitchen, there needs, at least, to be a common theme to the flowers serving different purposes in the room. For example, spring bulbs could be the link: A large container of daffodils on a work surface or window ledge could be complemented by blue grape hyacinths in little jars on a table. Or, perhaps, a large vase of garden roses together with other summer flowers could be echoed by a smaller bowl of the same rose varieties on the table. A collection of small vases and jars with a few coordinating flowers in each could provide another answer, since they can be moved around from one place to another and in different groupings according to need. They might make up a window ledge design during the day, for instance, and then come into play as a dinner table display in the evening, when the curtains are drawn and the window area becomes insignificant.

If the cooking and eating space is large and needs to be visually divided into different areas, flowers can help to make the distinction. An eating area delineated by a floor rug in primary colors, say, could have its

character heightened by an arrangement in the same palette; the colors of the cooking area could be similarly reflected by flowers on a work surface. The functions of the room, which change between different areas and different times of the day, need to be thought about—arrangements should be as flexible as the life that is lived in this busy area of the home.

BELOW This earthenware jar appears artless, but in fact the blue and yellow and white irises pick up the colors of the hutch and its collection of painted ceramics.

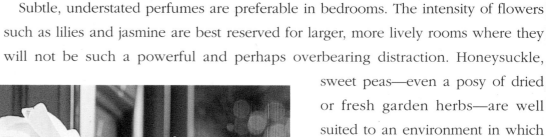

Bedrooms

Bedrooms are places of calm, relaxation, and sensuality, and flower arrangements should reflect these qualities. Overpowering or vibrant flowers are usually avoided in these tranquil settings—unless the character of the bedroom demands a similarly striking arrangement. In particular, flowers can be used to introduce their wonderful natural perfumes to these private retreats. What better welcome could there be to a guest bedroom than the gentle scent of lush roses or peonies infusing the room from a bedside table?

Subtle, understated perfumes are preferable in bedrooms. The intensity of flowers such as lilies and jasmine are best reserved for larger, more lively rooms where they will not be such a powerful and perhaps overbearing distraction. Honeysuckle, sweet peas—even a posy of dried or fresh garden herbs—are well suited to an environment in which to unwind and relax.

In the same way that perfume should be low-key and have a subtle impact, the colors and textures of bedroom flowers are best kept at a similar, soothing pitch. Calming whites, pale pinks, blues, and mauves are more conducive to rest than the vibrant influence of exciting reds, oranges, and yellows; and soft, full-petaled blooms of a velvety texture are more suitable than spiky, waxy flower heads. The two bedroom flower arrangements illustrated here fit the bill: The pure-white flowers of the potted cyclamen plant, with its heart-shaped leaves; and creamy white roses, soft and scented and

BELOW A bright white cyclamen flourishes next to a window, its snowy petals reflecting more sunlight into the room.

OPPOSITE Cream florist's roses are a gentle and romantic addition to a master bedroom, positioned to exude their perfume as partners fall asleep.

Bedrooms

in a simple, stable glass vase. Both are pretty and romantic, but neither is overpowering or distracting in rooms with plain walls and calm blue-green decorations and bed linen.

Country-style bedrooms that make use of traditional floral wallpapers and chintz curtains may demand arrangements that are a little more emphatic; really subtle whites might simply get lost amid the general decoration of the room. However, the colors of chintz usually become subdued with time—faded by the light over the years or even designed to imitate the same effect—and the flowers should not try to shout any louder. Spring and summer garden blooms in pinks and blues are perfect here, and are in any case the original inspiration for many of the patterns of the chintzes and wall coverings.

Bedrooms are often cramped spaces, and the positioning of flower arrangements needs to be thought about. The bedside table, or a dresser table or chest of drawers, is the obvious position for a vase. It is important that it is not too tall or top heavy; a sleepy hand reaching over to an alarm clock needs to be able to bump into the flowers without risking an early-morning disaster, for example. In addition, the arrangement of flowers itself should not be so frail that brushing past it will ruin the position of its flowers or even shatter the delicate petals of the blooms. In small rooms, a bowl with floating blooms can be a good solution for a dressing table; or a low container with a florist's foam base can work well beside the bed, as there is then no risk of spilling water.

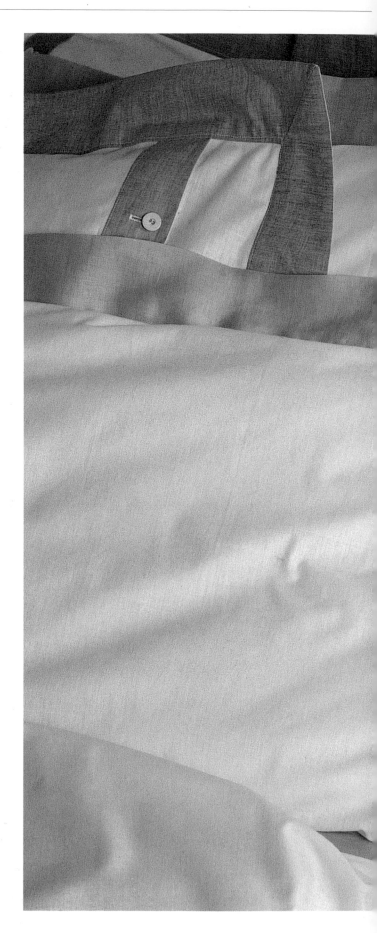

RIGHT *English summer-garden colors are present here in the pastel borders of the pillows and sheets, in the rose-spray wallpaper, and in the vase of real garden flowers on the bedside table.*

Bedrooms

ABOVE *Gardenia augusta 'Veitchiana' makes the most glamorous bedside companion—pure white, smoothly textured, and with a fabulous perfume.*

BELOW *Christmas roses arranged in a moss-lined glass bowl are pretty, happy flowers for a bedroom.*

On a slightly grander scale, bedrooms with connecting bathrooms can use flowers as a major design feature. Such rooms are likely to be larger than average, perhaps with space for a fairly large arrangement, such as the tulips on the blanket box illustrated opposite. An adjacent bathroom might then use a single tulip bloom in a smaller glass vase to continue the look right through the suite.

In a loft apartment or other completely open-plan living space, the bedroom is sometimes visible from the living areas, perhaps as a raised gallery above the main space. Here the flowers throughout the apartment can be designed either to unify areas with different living functions, or to distinguish between the different areas.

Finally, regardless of any rules of design or esthetics, the bedroom may be the place where you want to have your favorite flowers or plants for your own, solitary enjoyment. For many people, the bedroom is the only escape from the buzz of family life, where it is possible to indulge personal tastes and idiosyncrasies.

RIGHT *A large bunch of tulips in a glass jar can bend and curl and go with the flow. The white heads and pale green foliage coordinate exactly with the colors used elsewhere in the bedroom.*

Index of scented plants

We no longer regard our homes as predominantly functional machines for living. The twenty-first-century house is also a retreat, a welcoming environment for essential relaxation and recuperation from the stresses of everyday life. We expect our homes to pander to all our senses, to sight, hearing, touch, taste, and smell. No amount of imported perfume, in the form of scented candles or room sprays, can begin to approach the quality of naturally scented plants and flowers.

ABOVE *Broom (Genista sp.) has a rather sweet fragrance, and its spiky branches with small, pealike flowers can also be useful to add height and volume to an arrangement. The variety shown here has delicate, white flowers, but broom also commonly has yellow and red flowers.*

ABOVE Lilium speciosum *'Stargazer' is now a florist's favorite, valued for its dramatic blooms and for its heady, strong perfume. A few stems of the flower can fill the whole home with their scent.*

ABOVE *Clockwise from top: A collection of scented garden roses: Rosa 'Fritz Nobis,' Rosa 'Gloire de Dijon,' Rosa rugosa 'Alba,' Rosa 'Etoile de Hollande,' and Rosa 'Blessings.'*

ABOVE *From left to right: Strong springtime perfume comes from freesia, lilac (Syringa sp.), and hyacinth. These perfumes need to be enjoyed on their own, and the flowers should not be mixed together in an arrangement.*

RIGHT *Clockwise from right: Narcissi, Christmas box* (Sarcococca hookeriana), *florist's rose, Easter lily* (Lilium longiflorum), *sweet pea* (Lathyrus odoratus), *and crab apple* (Malus sp.).

ABOVE *The acacias are a species of evergreen shrubs and trees with tiny, globular flowers, usually yellow, that have a honeyed scent and pleasing, spiky leaves.*

ABOVE *Mexican orange blossom* (Choisya ternata) *has a strong, sweet—some might say sickly—perfume. The plant is favored primarily for its waxy, dark-green foliage.*

LEFT *Clockwise from left: Honeysuckle* (Lonicera sp.), Virburnum tinus, *wormwood* (Artemisia sp.), *myrtle* (Myrtus communis), *geranium* (Pelargonium sp.), *and carnation* (Dianthus sp.).

ABOVE Pelargonium graveolens *'Lady Plymouth' is grown for its sweetly scented, pungent leaves. The leaves are pale green, with frilly, white edges.*

183

Naturally perfumed bowl

No two people have the same perfume preferences, and this scented bowl could work equally well with other flowers and foliage according to your nose. When making any arrangement that mixes scented flowers, however, it is important to judge whether the perfumes will combine well. This is an art in itself—as any professional perfumier would tell you—and can only really be done by experimenting, putting ideas together, and sniffing at the end result. Too many strong scents can make the effect sickly sweet rather than light and refreshing.

1 Wire mesh is cut slightly larger than a wide-lipped bowl, placed over the top and bent over the edge to secure it. Strip sprigs of pearl everlasting of their lower leaves and trim the stems so that leaf sprays about 4in (10cm) in length remain. Insert at intervals all around the bowl.

2 Treat sprigs of purple sage the same way, inserting them around the bowl between the pearl everlasting.

3 Insert double sprigs of variegated apple mint in three groups inside the circle of foliage.

4 Secure six or seven stems of lady's mantle loosely with a rubber band and push them through into the center.

5 Put in small bunches of deadnettles between the lady's mantle and the outer circle of foliage.

6 Make small bunches of curly-leaved mint and push them down into the arrangement to fill any gaps.

7 Insert scented geranium leaves to fill gaps and finish with a few stems of lavender in the middle.

Flowers & entertaining

A table set for dinner—or even a tray set for breakfast in bed—always looks complete and enticing when flowers are a part of the setting. Flowers signal that a special occasion is underway, or they simply offer a warm welcome to all guests who enter the home.

Table decorations

Even the simplest table setting is brought to life by the addition of flowers—a bright selection cut from the garden, perhaps. But when the flowers on the table are part of a specific design, their impact can be really spectacular. A clever centerpiece arrangement can provide accents of color in a neutral table design, or can pick up the colors in the surrounding napkins, china, glasses, or tablemats. Tiny individual vases can grace each place around the table flowers or foliage can be tied around napkins; or the whole table can even be strewn with petals for an excessive, indulgent, and exotic effect. A table set for entertaining would seem incomplete without flowers or foliage of some kind.

The floating world

For evening meals, flowers often find their place on the table alongside the candles that are used to make a soft, flattering light for the diners. Candles and flowers combined are powerful mood makers, creating atmospheres that are anything from exciting and exotic to warm and pretty. The two candle and flower arrangements pictured here are both cheerful and calming at the same time. They are also very easy to achieve—especially important when you might be busy preparing food. Floating candles on water introduces a sense of peace to a table, and a touch of the Orient, and the brilliant flower tints prevent the idea from becoming solemn.

RIGHT Brilliant color from mixed gerberas makes a loud, fun statement, perfect for creating a party mood for this table, which is lit with floating candles in both contrasting and coordinating colors.

Table decorations

RIGHT *A thoroughly contemporary take on a floating theme uses colorful and scented flowers and foliage in translucent plastic bowls. High color contrast is achieved with pink on yellow and scarlet on turquoise.*

Table decorations

In the first design on pages 188–9, individual floating candles swim in small glass bowls scattered around the center of a table. Flowers are simply strewn among them, their bright colors reflecting back and forth in the candlelit water and glass. The second arrangement uses one large glass bowl—it need not be sophisticated, a mixing bowl will do—in which to float candles and flower heads together. Although here the daisy-like flowers of spray chrysanthemums are chosen, almost any variations on the theme would work. The design could be of foliage alone, well-shaped leaves and sprigs of herbs, for example, or of a pleasant mass of wildflowers—floating heads of buttercups and lawn daisies would be charming and colorful. It is best, however, to choose flowers with open forms that will present their faces upward, because the shape of a flower will be lost if it slumps down onto its side.

The scented table

Introducing perfume to the table with flowers and foliage can be lovely, although care must be taken that the scents used are not overpowering or in too great a contrast to the food that you have chosen. One solution is to decorate the table with the same herbs that you are using in the kitchen. Bunches of rosemary, sage, thyme, or mint, for example, will bring a fresh hint of the menu to the table before the food arrives. Illustrated opposite is a bunch of herbs tied around a napkin. Everybody loves to be given flowers, and personal bunches like this, however

OPPOSITE A bunch of fragrant herb flowers and leaves is attached to a napkin with a length of tied cord. The table setting is medieval in style, and the herb posy is in keeping with the historical idea.

LEFT This floral table style is pretty, but escapes being too sentimental by its strong contrast with the pure-white, undecorated tablecloth.

Table decorations

ABOVE *A traditional table centerpiece is the last word in elegance—creamy-white flowers with an accent of regal purple arranged in a silver vase.*

RIGHT *This is a brilliant example of designing well with color: The blue-green foliage of mock orange pot plants matches tablecloth and goblets, and the orange berries accent the fringes of the napkins and the pillows in the background.*

OPPOSITE *Contemporary minimal chic is given the edge with extravagant vases of red tulips. The rectangular vases are in keeping with the tableware—round ones would ruin the effect.*

modest, are very welcoming, making guests feel that they have your individual attention. The decorative idea can be carried across the whole table, with a central arrangement of herbs and perhaps a larger vase incorporating them elsewhere in the room.

Color and form

Some of the most dramatically successful table flowers are those that introduce startling splashes of contrasting color to the overall design of the setting. A plain white tablecloth and white tableware has an intensified gleam when it contrasts with, say, a bowl of blue hyacinths or a slim vase of brilliant red gerberas. Alternatively, flower colors can coordinate, toning with the colors of the china, or matching the shades of checked tablemats, so that the whole design has a look of consistency and care.

Table flowers can create illusions, too. A formal flower arrangement, perhaps of lilies or irises, can dignify the simplest dining area, giving it a newfound elegance, and an abundant, spilling vase of garden roses can make an ordinary pasta meal appear lavish—without seeming pretentious. If your entertaining budget is tight, it is still worth spending part of it cleverly at the flower shop, or devoting a thoughtful quarter of an hour to snipping from the garden, and making an appealing arrangement. Table flowers make all the difference.

Eating outside

meal eaten alfresco is inevitably slightly informal, a little closer to nature. While we can modify the heat and light and air in a room inside, we do not have so much control in the open air—wind and mosquitoes, sunshine and showers are all beyond our power and will intervene to sabotage even the most rigorous plan. Flower arrangements on outdoor table settings would look faintly ridiculous if, then, they were designed to be too controlled and formal. Rather, they need to go with the flow along with the elements and encapsulate the freedom of nature.

They do, nevertheless, need to be striking and dominant if they are to receive any notice in the outside world of the backyard or terrace, where other plants are in abundant competition. If they are too modest and subtle, they will simply disappear into the natural backdrop. A careful design balancing act is required.

The surefire way to achieve notice for the flowers and focus for the outdoor table setting is to coordinate the flower colors with those of the rest of the table. Visually, this will pull the table together and allow it to stand out against its naturally chaotic

BELOW *Lime green (brighter than the surrounding garden) with orange and red making an exciting contrast with the pink garden flowers are followed through to all the elements of this table setting.*

surroundings. Even so, the colors used can echo those in the yard or on the terrace, emphasizing the pink of roses, say, or perhaps the brilliant red of potted geraniums. Colors from the red/pink/orange band of the spectrum work particularly well as the basis of outdoor designs because they contrast directly with green, the predominant color of the setting. A red tablecloth and coordinating flowers and tableware will be instantly striking on the lawn or underneath a shady tree.

ABOVE *A shiny metal pail containing a margarita daisy plant works well with a mosaic terrace table and brightens a simple lunch for two. The shiny pail echoes the garden setting, and is decorative in its own right.*

Eating outside

ABOVE *Dark-pink and yellow flowers and matching tablecloth provide contrast without too much drama for a traditional, romantic table underneath an apple tree.*

OPPOSITE *The pale greens and whites of this design are unobtrusive, letting the flowerpot of garden blooms become a gentle focal point.*

Garden flowers

As a general rule, it is best to avoid using florist's flowers for outdoor arrangements. Unless the garden itself contains exotic and stately species, they will look stiff and out of place. Flowers cut from the garden, or wildflowers, look much more at home outside. Backing them with plenty of airy foliage relates the flowers in an arrangement to the yard, where the flowers are seen in exactly this way, among the greenery.

Similarly, it is not appropriate to use elaborate and formal vases and containers for outdoor arrangements. Stick with the slightly informal atmosphere that outdoor meals create. Such events provide the perfect opportunity to employ the more unusual items in your store of containers—glass jars and pitchers, enamel pails, terracotta pots, and baskets, for example. In particular, watch out for containers with detailed patterns. These will rarely work well in an outdoor setting. They simply end up looking lost and rather pathetic among the elaborate (and infinitely finer) natural patterns of leaves, light, and shadows. It is preferable to use plain surfaces, or painted ones with very bold, perhaps geometric, patterning. Pots and pitchers made of natural materials, and with distinctive surface textures, look just right outdoors.

Finally, containers used for outdoor arrangements should be sturdy enough to withstand the elements. Slender little vases that are likely to blow over in the wind would be hopeless. If necessary, the bottom of a container can be weighted down by the addition of a few pebbles or glass marbles under the water so it will stand firm on the table.

Potted plants

Forget that sad old aspidistra languishing in a dusty room. Contemporary potted plants overflow with graceful foliage and bring window ledges alive with blooming color. Added to this, modern containers are a far cry from the dingy plastic flower pots of a few decades ago. It's time to take a fresh look at potted plants.

Matching pots with plants

Fashions change fast in flower arranging, and this fact is seen most strikingly in the changing styles of potted, or indoor, plants. Potted plants are positively born again. Once items of stern, green foliage left to look down sadly from the top of high shelves or slowly molder in unused fireplaces, they are now must-have chic accessories in the most ultramodern of interiors.

The pot part of such an accessory is now as fundamental to the style as the plant growing in it. If the two are complementary, a chic look is achieved, but if they are not, the result is seen as old-fashioned and perhaps even embarrassing. It is easy to see a potted plant as an easy option to fill a dead corner, but in fact it needs more design thought than many might at first imagine.

Indoor gardens

Living in an apartment has one major drawback— the lack of a yard or, often, any outdoor space. Some people seem only too pleased to be rid of the headache of taming the wild, but many of us yearn for the benefits of the natural world in some form or another. Potted plants provide an answer, acting as miniature gardens on window ledges, coffee tables, edges of bathtubs, and kitchen cabinets—in fact, anywhere with a bit of free flat space. Potted plants don't need to be flowers. Stylish little lawns and patches of moss can flourish in earthy terracotta pots or galvanized metal boxes. Such containers are understated, clean-cut, and natural looking—the idea of a stylized garden is not conjured up by a decorated

BELOW Bright white heather shrugs off its traditional tartan image to glimmer fashionably against metal and smooth white and gray pebbles.

OPPOSITE A glass cake stand hosts a new kind of delicacy—terracotta pots planted with mind-your-own-business plants that carry a mass of tiny, orange berries.

Matching pots with plants

plant holder or a plastic flower pot. Minimalist interiors, stripped of any clutter, have an eastern feel, and their mossy or low-growing fern or moss plants give the appearance of a sort of western bonsai garden.

Fashion for potted flowers, as opposed to foliage, has also become more exotic. Geraniums that were once reserved for the terrace outside now bring a touch of the Mediterranean into the home, and the popular chrysanthemum has been ousted by its modernist cousins, the gerbera family. Their pots are also carefully chosen. They may be customized, or perhaps visibly lined with moss—inside a wire mesh or, most fashionably, inside a glass vase, preferably a square or rectangular one.

In any event, the plants themselves are carefully tended. Shabby leaves and dead blooms are promptly trimmed away. Potted plants have now become elegant decorative accessories, treated with due respect.

BELOW *Not a blemish is to be found on this healthy geranium, given an outdoor appearance by its wire basket of moss.*

OPPOSITE *A gerbera acquires its own designer pot, painted in a checkerboard that sets off the vibrant, orange flowers and bright-green foliage.*

The window ledge

The window ledge, outside or in, is the obvious situation for hardy potted plants, particularly flowering ones that will soak up the sunlight to feed the colors of their petals. It also acts as the dividing line between inside and out, and by placing growing plants on the window ledge you can create a link, and an easy transition, between the natural world and the artifice of the interior. Plants on an outside ledge can be glimpsed from inside, and vice versa. It is even possible to have the same plants, perhaps arranged differently and in different pots both inside and out, to create continuity.

ABOVE A painted ceramic bowl is planted with delicate pink primulas that can grow equally well outside. Placed on a tiled kitchen sill, it is a reminder of the great outdoors.

Many potted plants, kept well watered, flourish on a window ledge, whereas the lives of cut flowers are shortened by exposure to the full glare of light and heat. Some potted species do, however, require partial shade and may find their place on a north-facing sill, away from a direct draft.

If the world outside the window is not as attractive and natural as you might like, there may be a need to screen it rather than highlight it, and to pull the focus toward a more exotic interior. The startling, attention-seeking amaryllis opposite does just this with its dramatic scarlet flowers. It is thoroughly well dressed, right down to its highly fashionable glass vase, filled with gravel and topped with stylish, smoothly finished seashore pebbles. The plant is natural enough, but its treatment is a piece of up-to the-minute interior design.

RIGHT Auriculas have recently become fashion pin-ups—possibly because the "faces" of the blooms have so much character. They look best planted singly, with pots grouped together.

LEFT *The amaryllis grows from a magically rewarding bulb. What at first appears to be a grubby onion grows fast and bursts into huge and colorful bloom.*

Grouping pots

A plant placed in splendid isolation automatically becomes something of a focal point. This may be exactly what is required of a spectacular specimen, but more modest potted plants may look rather sad and insignificant on their own. Grouping pots of the same plants or a mixture of different ones can give each a greater importance and can result in a rich display.

The *Primula obconica* displayed in the green earthenware pitchers opposite look companionable and definitive in a way that a solitary plant would not. The different sizes of the two pitchers that contain them (plastic flowerpots have been slid down inside the rims of the pitchers) add a pleasing element of variety. Similarly, the collection of Cape primroses (*Streptocarpus*) in terracotta pots pictured below make a bold statement that would be lost if they were displayed one by one.

While a cut flower arrangement can be carefully constructed to suit its situation in the home, so that height, width, span, colors, and textures are all designed to fit, growing plants cannot be tamed in the same way. Although it is possible to select the best scale and type of potted plant for a certain position, many, particularly the flowering plants, are best seen in groups. This corresponds to the planting of a

OPPOSITE *The dark-green, shiny glaze of these earthenware pitchers does not attempt to compete with the primulas, but makes the most of the contrasting delicate, pink flowers.*

LEFT *All the containers used for this group of Cape primroses are ordinary terracotta garden pots, but they are all slightly different in shape and size, making the grouping more lively.*

211

Grouping pots

ABOVE *A kitchen windowsill herb garden is made into a decorative accessory with the use of a matching collection of silver-painted pots.*

OPPOSITE *A lively mixture of flowering plants and ferns on a terrace is given coherence by metal containers all decorated with gold, geometric patterns.*

RIGHT *A pairing of moss-lined wire mesh "pots" of lavender and safflowers are, in fact, carefully designed cut-flower arrangements masquerading as plants.*

yard, where perennials or annuals are planted in groups of three to five in order to make a decent impact—one pelargonium alone in a flowerbed, for example, is almost invisible.

This theory also applies to the planting of terraces, patios, and balconies. Pots of different sizes and shapes, containing flowers and foliage that are complementary to each other and to the surroundings, create a much better visual effect than a few isolated pots strewn around at a distance from each other. Interestingly, each individual plant stands out better if it is in a group than it does if it is seen on its own; the contrasting colors and textures of others in the group give it definition.

There is great fun to be had in choosing the containers for groups of plants. All can be exactly the same to create a formal, contemporary look; all might be different but linked by color; or all might be the same shape and material, but in various sizes. Members of a group of pots can be changed around to achieve a different display, or when one plant comes into its full flowering and another begins to droop.

Training potted climbers

Climbing and trailing plants have a special delicacy and appeal, and it would be a pity to rule them out as indoor plants because of their growth habits. Small climbers and trailers can be grown successfully in pots, but they do need a little help—something to cling to. They can even be grown on a miniature trellis, perhaps to be placed against an interior wall in imitation of a garden design. However, seriously invasive plants are best kept outdoors.

Jasmine has pretty white flowers, dainty foliage, and the added advantage of an intense, heady perfume that can fill a room in which it is grown. With care in its planting, training, watering, and feeding, jasmine will flourish inside.

BELOW A stephanotis and an ivy remain comfortable trained around their wire hoops and thrive in the humid atmosphere of a bathroom.

1 Potted jasmine plants are usually sold with a wire hoop support in place. As the plant grows, a single wire is not adequate for the growth, since the plant's tendrils only have the opportunity to wind back and forth.

2 Unwind the tendrils of the plant carefully from the wire support and hang them gently over the side. Then remove the wire, which will be pushed down into the earth in the pot.

3 Plant the lower stakes of a wooden frame into the pot toward one side, then carefully weave the hanging tendrils through the trellis. As the plant grows, gaps in the trellis will be filled.

Candlelight

The moving, living flame of a candle gives an inimitable depth of light and shadow to flowers arranged alongside. The age-old combination of candlelight and flowers or foliage immediately spells romance. The magical effect is seductive enough to melt the hardest heart or to put the most energetic person at perfect ease.

Candles for the table

ABOVE *Thyme growing in the garden is at first glance an unlikely-looking candidate for candle decoration.*

A dinner table lit with candles is intimate; the flickering flames pull the attention of the diners into the restricted circle of light that they produce. Held in grand candlesticks, candles also bring a formality to a table, and used alone or in low holders they are modest. Candles combined with flowers, however, are mutually complementary: The candlelight playing on the foliage and blooms emphasizes the fact that they are living things; and the textures, shapes, and colors of the plants reflect the light of the candles and increase their sense of movement.

Candles have regained a huge popularity in recent years. Once wholly functional as a way of lighting the home, they were gratefully discarded with the advent of electricity, but now that we take such technology for granted, we have a desire for some of the qualities of the antique. Whole stores are now devoted to the sale of candles in every conceivable size, shape, color, and perfume—they have become designer items.

Floral designers have been quick to see the opportunities to work with candles in new ways, providing them with new decorative guises to suit modern table settings. Candles are wrapped with leaves or herbs or twigs, sunk into tiny metal pails with garden flowers, floated in finger bowls with a few stylish blooms, and given gourds or apples as bases. Instead of simply having one or a group of candles at the center of a table, individual candles may be

LEFT *A small, sturdy, white candle is decorated with a collar of thyme stalks, tied with garden twine.*

OPPOSITE *A contemporary Christmas table candle: A metal pot antiqued with gold, and ivy sprigs sprayed with gold paint, set off a central candle.*

Feature candles

placed next to each setting or small votive candles might be used all around the room—arranged in a neat regimental line along the window ledge or across a mantel shelf, for example.

This does not mean that more conventional flower and candle table arrangements have gone out of vogue. Decorative displays at the center of a table may now be in more up-beat containers, or include the blooms that are currently in fashion, and the candles themselves are chosen carefully from the huge variety available.

Feature candles

For a really grand meal or a lavish evening party, candles and flowers are guaranteed to provide the most glamorous of decorations, their flickering drawing the attention of guests. This is an opportunity to go over the top, to create a fantasy that will add magic to a party atmosphere.

BELOW *A more conventional treatment, but one employing the up-to-the-minute color combination of scarlet, lime green, and gray-blue.*

Larger and elaborate candle and flower decorations need a firm structure onto which they can be constructed. An existing candlestick or candelabra, made of metal rather than more fragile ceramic, is ideal, particularly if its shape presents a chance of hiding soaked florist's foam or little jars of water for cut flowers. In such cases, the flowers and foliage used to decorate the holder must be abundant and tightly packed so they cover the practical, unsightly elements of the arrangement altogether.

Candles in plant pots provoke the illusion of their growth, and automatically look fashionable. Flowers used around them in the pots will usually be cut, but perhaps arranged so they appear to be growing. There is no real reason, however, why a suitable candle cannot be placed in the center of a real potted plant, as long as it does not do any damage, for a temporary but renewable candle decoration.

OPPOSITE *Slender tapers appear to grow among a gentle arrangement of spring flowers for an Easter meal table.*

Feature candles

Even the backyard or garden shed can yield a whole host of unexpected treasures that can be used to make an unusual flower/candle arrangement. For example, place half a globe-shaped piece of florist's foam inside a simple terracotta flowerpot, and soak it lightly. Position a tall honeycomb candle in the center of the foam; then stand the pot on a large square of chicken wire. The chicken wire should be large enough to fold up around the flowerpot, extending well beyond and outward from the rim. Next add the foliage, any flexible type that is in season; for instance, variegated ivy, and trailing ivy (plain or variegated), berry twigs—complete with leaves—possibly some pine foliage, if it is available. Then make more of a feature of the berries: Press them into the florist's foam through the chicken wire, which will support their weight. For strong color accent, press some white roses into the foam, again securing their position by first passing them through the chicken wire. The wire will support any foliage that you trail or place along it, and can be bent this way, allowing you to balance the arrangement.

BELOW Candles are permanently set into terracotta flowerpots with plaster-of-Paris. Dried eucalyptus and roses are cleverly wired around cardboard tubes that are then slipped down over the candles.

OPPOSITE This romantic candelabra has been achieved with a central cube of florist's foam and chicken wire to provide water and support for the flowers and foliage that hide it from view.

Winter celebrations

Special occasions during the fall and winter months seem incomplete without the literal and metaphoric warmth of open fires and candlelight to create an inviting interior. These seasonal celebrations are equally inconceivable without the decorative accessories of fruits, evergreens, berries, and fir cones brought inside to decorate the home. The two elements combine beautifully to create an atmosphere of richness and of welcoming retreat from the cold.

The two candle arrangements illustrated here demonstrate opposite ends of the spectrum of ways in which the elements can be put together successfully. On the left is a highly structured feature of dried flowers, fruits, cones, and moss that takes some time to make and is intended to last the season and have a traditional appeal. On the right, twigs of holly are simply wound around the arms of a glass candelabra as temporary, instant decoration. This will only take minutes to do, but cleverly combines the shiny textures of glass and waxy holly leaves, which are then intensified in the light of the candle flames.

This difference proves the point that you do not require advanced skills of craftsmanship to decorate successfully with flowers and plants: The simple is often as beautiful as the more complex. The essential talent lies in the looking, in being able to see what will look good in a certain situation and having the courage to experiment until you achieve a well-designed end.

BELOW A Christmas centerpiece is constructed bit by bit in an everyday cake pan, using fresh, dried, and synthetic elements to create a rich and fruitful effect.

OPPOSITE Holly climbing a glass candelabra is one part of a designer's scheme that repeats the use of holly and glassware across a Christmas table.

Winter celebrations

RIGHT *Sparkling Christmas candles (plain, white ones with applied gold leaf and scratched pattern) give an extra glow to a surrounding arrangement of rowan berries and pomegranates.*

Natural candleholders

These informal candleholder arrangements are simple in style, but are neverthe-less attractive—they are also extremely easy to make. One idea is to fill a small flowerpot with a large candle surrounded by a collar of just leaves, or both foliage and flowers. The other idea, highly fashionable right now, is to disguise a glass jar holder so a candle appears to be parceled up with leaves. Either of these candle arrangements is perfect for an informal supper table or, if a number of holders are made, for lighting an entire living room for a party. It is not necessary to use the exact ingredients shown here, since many other flowers and leaves would also look pretty; you can simply use whatever is easily at hand. Choose your ingredients according to the time of year as well as your personal tastes. In spring you might add a few fresh buds, and in the fall some sprigs of colorful berries.

1 Line a small flowerpot with plastic and press a cube of soaked florist's foam inside so it protrudes just above the rim. Tape three slim, split-bamboo stakes around the candle and push them down into the center of the foam.

2 Push several short sprigs of eucalyptus into the foam around the flowerpot, then add as many short stems of safflowers as is needed to make a pleasing circular design. View the arrangement from all sides, as well as from above, to check that the flowers and foliage are evenly placed.

3 Make sure the leaves and flowers cover both the tape securing the stakes around the candle and the rim around the flowerpot where the foam protrudes above it. Gently ease a little of the arrangement over the edge if any of the foam is showing through.

Natural candleholders

1 Glue glossy evergreen leaves of similar size (camellia is used here) around a small glass jar, making sure the decorative edges of the leaves point up.

OPPOSITE *The method described on the previous pages is used here for a flowerpot candle surrounded by scented geranium leaves. As the lighted candle warms the leaves, their fragrance is enhanced.*

2 Trim around the base of the jar with scissors so the leaves are snipped to the same level.

3 Tie the leaves around in the middle with a raffia bow and insert a small candle to fit neatly inside the jar.

Growing indoor bulbs

Those first, courageous blooms that push through the winter soil bring such a rush of relief that we cannot resist introducing their life and vigor into the house. We relish the bright, clear colors and sharp, uncomplicated perfumes of snowdrops, hyacinths, jonquils, and daffodils as they slowly open, heralding the spring.

Tulips

ABOVE The smooth texture and strong outlines of tulips contrast well with the furry twigs of pussy willow (Salix sp.) that is found at the same time of the year.

RIGHT This is an exercise in color contrast, easily achieved with the varied and vivid hues of tulips: Yellow and green are brought into focus with a dash of bright red.

OPPOSITE An original, graphic black and white table setting is provided with the strong contrast of magenta tulips, each in an individual plastic, spring-water bottle.

Tulips have the unique ability of arranging themselves. Within days—or sometimes hours—those tight-budded, straight-stemmed blooms have opened wide and twisted and contorted into waves and curves that look out from a vase in all directions. This can be a frustration for the flower arranger who has a specific scheme in mind, but really the character of this extraordinary flower, valued for centuries, should be enjoyed in all its guises, its independence applauded.

The glamour of tulips dates back in the West to the mid-sixteenth century, when travelers to Turkey talked of the exotic flower so prized by the Turks. However most people associate the tulip's history with the mania for the flower that existed in Holland in the 1630s, when it was said that a single, rare bulb could change hands for the price of a substantial house. Unusual tulip cultivars—quixotic, multicolored, striped, and petal-stained—were the most sought after esthetic commodity in seventeenth-century Holland. The beauty of many of these tulips was captured in still-life flower paintings of the period, executed by the finest painters.

Although we no longer hold the bulb in quite such reverence, interest in tulips has continued since, to the extent that there are now more than four thousand varieties of garden tulips available. Among this huge number are tulips of almost any color—including purples so dark that they pass as black, and whites that are as white as any flower can be. The bulbs also throw up blooms in many shapes—from

Tulips

OPPOSITE *This Easter table is awash with cheerful spring flowers, but the tulips—graceful and elegant, leaning over like dancers—take the central position.*

BELOW *Scarlet parrot tulips curl themselves into sinuous forms in a creamware pitcher. The arrangement is full of movement and exoticism.*

the slender-waisted points favored in the East to blowsy, rounded cup shapes; and from chiseled petals to elaborately torn and ragged edges. Added to the panoply of varieties now are miniature tulips, often grown in rockeries, in which all this exoticism is condensed into a tiny frame.

Tulips very often look their best arranged on their own, rather than as part of a bunch of mixed flowers; and further, the intricate colors and patterns of the flower heads are best seen if only one variety of tulip is used. A vase of tulips can deliver a dynamite hit of pure, brilliant color, particularly the red and yellow varieties, that would have less impact if it were tempered with other shades. Other tulips can be subtle and sinuous, such as the palest of pale yellows and the warmest apricot and beige. Whatever color you choose, best let the tulip have its way and unfold its character in the vase, revealing a contrasting star at its center or a surprising stripe along the backs of its petals. There is no flower that flaunts its grand past quite as outrageously as a tulip.

Hyacinths

ABOVE *By planting hyacinth bulbs in two matching rows along a low rectangular container, a modern take on the traditional basket of spring bulbs is created.*

We value the spring tulips for their color, but we turn to the hyacinth for the marvelous, heady perfume of the new year. In the early months, countless households bring their bulbs out from a dark cupboard just as the green tip is emerging and watch them open up and scent the air. The simplest flower arrangement of all is, perhaps, a specially shaped molded glass bottle that contains a single hyacinth bulb, its white roots curling through the water and its large flowered stem above. Blue, either an intense, dark shade or a light, pastel one, is still a favorite color for hyacinths, but they are now available to buy in an increasing range of colors, including white, yellow, orange, salmon, purple, and mauve.

By Easter, the florist's shelves are lined with moss-filled baskets of flowering hyacinth bulbs and the contemporary equivalent of glass and metal containers. Most extravagant of all is to buy cut hyacinths (with the bulbous end of the stem still intact) from a florist to arrange in a vase.

Although the hyacinth cannot lay claim to eminence equal to the tulip's, the bulb was also avidly developed in seventeenth-century Holland and had a thriving market value of its own. It comes originally from the Middle East, but was cultivated in

1 Hyacinth bulbs are planted with their tops protruding from the medium, ready to be kept in a dark place for 6 to 10 weeks.

2 When their shoots reach an inch or so in height, they can be brought into a warm, light position and surrounded with moss to trap the moisture.

239

Hyacinths

ABOVE *Powerful fragrance is released into a room from a substantial basket of indoor forced hyacinths—here in a wonderful deep purple-blue hue.*

Europe by the ancient Greeks and Romans. It was much admired in the eighteenth and nineteenth centuries (hence the contemporaneous popularity of the English name Hyacinth for girls), ornamenting women's hats as well as their gardens. The flower was particularly fashionable in mid-eighteenth-century France, as a result of Madame de Pompadour's taste for hyacinths in huge abundance in the gardens and in the halls of Versailles.

The smaller grape hyacinths were a popular ordinary garden flower in England through the early and mid-twentieth century, used to edge flowerbeds and to grow in little clumps in spare patches of soil. The grape hyacinth fell out of fashion for a while, but is now back with a vengeance, grown inside in little aluminum or striped ceramic pots. Its formality and clear-blue color complement the clean lines of modern interiors well. And we should save a thought for the hyacinth's wild equivalent, the bluebell, which carpets woodlands with an ethereal blue that is breathtaking.

OPPOSITE BELOW *A row of pots like miniature trashcans stand sentry along a small window ledge, filled with cut grape hyacinths. This idea would work well in a kitchen or bathroom, and would provide a delightful touch in a guest's bedroom.*

LEFT *No childhood would seem complete without growing a hyacinth in a specially designed jar, where water does the job of soil, providing nutrition for the roots.*

241

Narcissi & daffodils

Behind the innocent white face of narcissus lies a dark soul. In spite of their jolly appearance and sweet scent, narcissi are named after the Greek word for numbness, in reference to the narcotic properties of the plant. The bulbs are poisonous, containing a paralyzing alkaloid. The intrigue of this spotless-looking spring flower is further deepened by the Greek myth of Narcissus, the youth who was transfixed by the reflection in a pool of his own beautiful face, a forbidden obsession that cost him his immortality. The association persisted: In nineteenth-century England, narcissi symbolized vanity.

The narcissi family

The flower was first cultivated by the Romans and remains today, in all its hundreds of varieties, one of the most popular garden and cut flowers. Tiny, creamy-white jonquils are valued for their intense perfume; white narcissi have trumpets in palest peach and lemon or in brilliant orange and yellow; and daffodils now follow suit in every shade from white to almost orange.

The connotations of the daffodil are happy, particularly since their mood-lifting effect upon the young William Wordsworth. Such was their golden

LEFT Narcissus papyraceus *is a stunning, delicate, star-shaped variety with tiny, peach corollas. The flower heads splay widely from elegant, slender stalks.*

RIGHT *A row of coordinating pastel-colored ceramic pots lined up along an outside window ledge modernize simple, small daffodils and provide visual impact.*

Narcissi & daffodils

power that his poem in their praise is now arguably his best known—although by no means his best literary—work. He was right, of course: It is impossible to see such a triumphant yellow display of thousands of blooms blowing gently in the breeze without feeling considerably restored. By the fact of their jolly appearance, and by association, the same can be said about a small bunch of daffodils suddenly enlivening a room in early spring.

Curiously, narcissi and daffodils bring out strong opinions. Some people love the astringent scent of jonquils, while others find the perfume almost repugnant. Some love all the new varieties of the flower on the market, with their frilly trumpets and pastel or bright shades, while others are firmly of the view that narcissi should be white and daffodils should be yellow. Certainly, the ascetic minimalists among us value the white varieties as assured good taste for interiors; and the traditionalists in our midst stick to daffodil bulbs growing in a mossy basket. It doesn't matter. The fact is that there is now a tremendous choice of bulbs and cut flowers to suit many situations in the garden and the house, and the narcissi family is hugely enjoyable.

OPPOSITE *A contemporary conservatory dining space, composed around white, gray, and green, is brightened by a large glass vase of white narcissi, marshaled straight up to the necks.*

BELOW *The traditional joy of spring: Happy little* narcissus *'tête-à-tête' in their old-fashioned wicker basket.*

Springtime blue and yellow

Blue and yellow is a popular color scheme for decorating, particularly of kitchens and informal dining rooms, and this spring arrangement would complement such an interior beautifully. The design could be varied according to the colors of the room in which it is to be displayed—it could, for example, feature blue and white flowers, or pink and white. To make the most of what is quite a complicated arrangement, though, choose a number of flowers that are strongly perfumed—like the hyacinths and yellow narcissi here.

1 Place a large bowl of water in the center of a decorative wreath —this one is composed of vine stems. Crumple chicken wire to fit inside the bowl.

2 Cover the chicken wire completely with pieces of moss. Insert single hyacinths and tied bunches of grape hyacinths on one side of the bowl.

3 Cut a hole in the chicken wire next to the blue flowers and insert a primrose plant, removed from its growing pot, with roots and moist soil ball in plastic wrap.

4 Decorate the sides of the arrangement with sprigs of ivy—green and variegated—cut so their stems can be pushed down into the water.

5 Continue to enhance the design and to fill gaps with narcissi, hyacinths, and grape hyacinths, until the finished result is a pleasing, natural-looking shape.

Decorating
with roses

The rose is the one flower that offers everything. It seems that among the hundreds of different varieties of rose are all the shapes, colors, textures, and perfumes of the entire flower world. The rose captures every mood, from purity to drama, from antique to modern.

249

White roses

RIGHT AND BELOW *Florist's blooms in cream and pure white are a more formal alternative to the free-flowering garden varieties, yet they retain a natural look.*

The rose is a prickly shrub or climber native to northern, temperate regions of the world. This prosaic description, though, belies the beauty and many associations of this most popular and emotive flower.

The rose played its part in Greek mythology, gaining its status as a symbol of love and desire, and of silence. The flower was favored by the Romans, who strewed city streets and banqueting halls with its petals at the height of their excesses, and ordered enormous rose gardens to supply their habit. Christianity at first rejected the flower, then gave in to its popularity and reinterpreted the pagan symbolism to represent the Virgin Mary, the "rose without thorns." The wars between the houses of Lancaster and York for the English crown between 1455 and 1485 saw the heraldry of the red rose for Lancaster and the white rose for York, so that the period is now known as the Wars of the Roses. And today, to have a variety of the thousands of roses cultivated each year named after you is a sure sign of success and fame in the modern world.

OPPOSITE *'Sanders' White Rambler' and 'Iceberg' are combined with lady's mantle and wisteria leaves for a table decoration for an outdoor meal.*

White roses

ABOVE *The addition of silvery foliage and blue-black berries to a small, white bowl of white roses intensifies their purity and glow by providing strong contrasts.*

RIGHT *Creamy florist's roses are relieved of their stiffness in an arrangement with a generous amount of background foliage.*

Everybody has a favorite rose, or a preferred type of the species, from old-fashioned single blooms, newly created show blooms, standard shrubs, or abundant climbers. The benefits of different colors, forms, growth habits, and fragrances are hotly disputed among rose growers and devotees. White and cream roses are valued by many for their purity and simplicity. Used as cut decoration, they are strongly associated with weddings and christenings, at which they represent purity, but the white and cream varieties are now commonly used in home arrangements.

Roses are available from the florist at any time of the year, but recently old-fashioned garden roses have regained their popularity. They do not always produce perfect specimen blooms like the purchased flowers, but they have a simplicity and form that is all the more beautiful for its imperfections—and they have wonderful fragrances that are often missing in highly cultivated and forced modern varieties.

White roses

OPPOSITE *For a full impact of summer fragrance, cream miniature roses are backed by jasmine. This heady mix would be lovely in a sunny living room.*

There are many white garden roses suitable for cutting for the house, chosen to suit tastes and planting position. Among those that are easy to find and to grow are *Rosa mulliganii,* which has single-petal flowers, long stems, and a delicious scent; the well-known (and sometimes wrongly maligned) 'Iceberg,' which flowers profusely and is a pure white, as its name suggests; 'Boule de Neige,' fragrant, with dense rosettes of petals and repeat flowering; and 'Sanders' White Rambler,' a lovely plant for trellises that flowers in late summer when other roses may have stopped.

Garden roses need to be cut early in the day, when the blooms are three-quarters open. Remove thorns—being careful not to prick your fingers—and lower leaves, then stand them up to their necks in cold water for a few hours before arranging. The stems need to be cut at a sharp angle, ideally when they are still submerged in water, to reveal as large a surface area as possible of the inner pith that absorbs water.

Any of the garden roses described above look wonderful arranged on their own, perhaps in a pale-green vase to add cool contrast to their brilliance, or for a room decorated in a similar palette. The addition of silver-green or lime-green foliage has a balancing effect, and can soften the appearance of formal blooms. Although many designers prefer to use roses alone in modernist arrangements, they combine well with some other summer flowers. White roses can look fantastic contrasted with the bright, deep blues of delphiniums and larkspur, for example. A mixed-color vase of comparatively small or tall summer flowers is brought into sharp focus by the incorporation of, say, three big-headed, white cabbage roses. And, of course, old-fashioned roses bring fragrance wherever they go.

BELOW *Ivory roses are given an antique feel by combining them with poppy seed heads in an old stoneware vase. The arrangement is supported by means of the small neck of the vase.*

Red roses

ABOVE *This miniature, pinkish-red rose, Rosa 'Rouletii,' can be grown successfully indoors in a pot to make a long-lasting room decoration.*

The red rose carries with it a symbolism that no other flower can now match. A bunch of red roses—particularly if they are dark, mysterious, and velvety—talk first and foremost of love and passion. Presented as a gift, there is no mistaking their message. Poets have for centuries evoked the rose to aid the metaphors of their feelings. "If love were what the rose is,/And I were like the leaf,/Our lives would grow together..." opines Swinburne in full Victorian flood. Fifty years later, though, Dorothy Parker had tired of the rose's easy message: "Why is it no one ever sent me yet/One perfect limousine, do you suppose?/Ah no, it's always just my luck to get/One perfect rose."

However, most of us cannot resist the sophisticated charms of the red rose. The queen of flower arrangers, Constance Spry, writing in 1937, made clear of the red rose that "used in mass there is no other flower which can add more beauty and adornment to a large festivity." She favored richly colored reds with a deep scent, and advised against combining the red rose with any sort of greenery. Her favorite treatment was an arrangement of dark crimson roses set off with purplish and slate-blue varieties. The best red roses, says Spry, are the very dark ones with almost a black sheen that will throw other reds into relief.

Constance Spry was a firm advocate of old-fashioned garden varieties of rose, which she thought had a much more desirable, natural habit when cut and arranged than the staunch florist's varieties. Among the many desirable garden red roses on offer today and suitable for cutting are the dark crimson 'Cardinal de Richelieu' and the slightly lighter, velvety 'Tuscany'; 'Crimson shower,' which has double crimson flowers and blooms throughout the summer; and the crimson patio rose, for growing in pots or as ground cover, called 'Festival.'

ABOVE Rosa *'Nicole' is a florist's variety that is available throughout the year, even at Christmas, when it can be arranged with shiny, evergreen foliage.*

LEFT *A small bowl makes the perfect container for the short stems of a terracotta red rose with soft-pink under-petals, and is used as a dining table decoration.*

Red roses

OPPOSITE *Red and pink garden roses, arranged with lady's mantle, complement a traditional living room.*

RIGHT *These scarlet roses have been carefully dried to preserve the full impact of their rich color, and are composed here with moss and seedheads in strongly contrasting greens.*

Red roses inevitably make a powerful statement. They may be elegant, voluptuous, dazzling, or romantic, but they are never subtle or understated. The mood they evoke is wide awake and demanding, rather than restful and calm. They need to be positioned with care; scarlet roses might not, for example, be at their best in a yellow room, although the darkest crimson might work well. A contrasting background room color, such as green or blue, will provide red roses with the best setting. It is all the mystery of red that is on display, and it needs to be strongly defined.

ABOVE *Pink and red roses of graduated tone that can be used together are, from the top: 'Chapeau de Napoléon,' 'Duc de Guiche,' and 'Celsiana.'*

Pastel colors

RIGHT 'Golden Showers' is a fragrant, double, clear-yellow climbing rose with blooms borne in clusters. It flowers through the summer and pales as it opens.

A mix of pastel-colored roses in a prettily patterned ceramic pitcher is an image that is strongly associated with summer in the country. The roses are gathered from the garden at random and displayed simply, perfuming the house and dropping their velvety petals onto an old oak table top.

The image works well in reality,

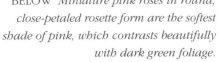

since the pastel shades of roses are often a similar tone and texture, so they coordinate well. Shades of pale pink, apricot, and primrose blend effortlessly, helped by the depths and shadows cast by their petals, so that an arrangement has a gentle, cloudy appearance. For this to succeed,

BELOW Miniature pink roses in round, close-petaled rosette form are the softest shade of pink, which contrasts beautifully with dark green foliage.

LEFT *An antique effect is achieved with this glass pitcher filled with large-headed, old-fashioned, double-petaled garden roses in pale pink and yellow.*

though, the shades must be really pale, as stronger colors would create a different effect and be more likely to clash in unintended ways.

Again, there are numerous garden varieties of roses that boast subtle, pastel shades and that will have a good lifespan when cut and brought inside. The profuse 'New Dawn' is one of the most understated and desirable of pastels—a soft bluish-pink rambler that flowers all summer long. 'Korresia' is a pale yellow, cluster-flowered bush rose with light-green foliage, and is ideal for growing in backyard flowerbeds and for cutting for displays around the house. A large bush rose, 'Rosemary Harkness,' has glossy, dark leaves and a sweet-scented, apricot flower.

Vibrant rose bowl

This arrangement is intended to make a big impact. Its mix of burgundy, orange, and red roses and berries is designed to be seen from above, where it appears like a starburst and is full of movement. Therefore, it would be suitable for an informal buffet party, for example. A similar style could be used for other colors—bright yellows and golds, for example—but the principle of contrasting the compact round forms of the roses with the spiky stems of the other plants remains the same.

1 Prepare a wide ceramic bowl with soaked florist's foam and form the basic structure of the design with short stems of fruiting hypericum.

2 Add short stems of shiny, dark-red cornus to about the same height, following around with a star shape in mind.

3 Add seven long stems of red-berried euphorbia to form a star radiating out from the center to the outside of the arrangement.

4 Add the roses all around, in varying lengths and grouped together fairly compactly rather than dotted about—this will give more impact of color and shape.

Decorative dried flowers

Introduction

We experience a sense of loss in the knowledge that a flower is ephemeral—that it blooms, withers, and dies within days, sometimes hours. This creates a feeling that if only we could preserve that beauty, keep it secure from decay, that a certain disappointment would be avoided.

These emotions, combined with a desire to continue to take pleasure in the color of cut flowers long after their flowering seasons have ended, are behind the long history and enduring appeal of drying and preserving flowers, foliage, grasses, seedheads, and other products of the natural world. The processes of preserving plants so they retain their good looks are exacting and time-consuming, but any effort on our part is offset by the long-lasting pleasure that they bring. Suddenly, flower arrangements can be in place for months rather than days.

Elements of the natural world

In this final section, arrangements in a range of styles of, first, dried flowers and, second, berries, seed pods, and grasses, are examined. Ways of combining each of them with other elements of the natural world, such as mosses, shells, stones, fruits, and twigs, are also suggested.

In particular, there is an emphasis here on dried flower and plant designs that are fresh and lively, arrangements that avoid the pitfall of merely being something to fill an empty corner and gather dust over the years. Fashions in flower arranging change fast, and nowhere is this fact more evident than in dried designs. This section therefore gives an overview of both the traditional and the very modern approaches to the art. It ends with a comprehensive index of plants from the garden, the countryside, and the florist that are suitable for drying and preserving.

LEFT *Flowers usually need to be dried hanging with the blooms down so the moisture runs to the flower heads during the process. An old wooden clothes dryer provides the perfect vehicle.*

RIGHT *An exotic-looking mixture of petals, seed heads, and foliage creates a stunning potpourri in a shallow glass bowl. The intensity of the colors remains intact.*

Floral
displays

Replenishing fresh flower arrangements weekly from the florist during the winter months can be a costly business. Careful drying or preserving of spring and summer flowers that retain their color well, however, is satisfying and economical. Dried flower arrangements can have an impact or a subtlety equal to that of fresh blooms. And they last all season.

Introducing the flowers

ABOVE *Pink and red flowers, coordinating with the neutral colors of grasses, give an idea of the exciting choice of plants available for thoughtful dried flower arrangements.*

Although the successful drying and preserving of flowers means that they retain the best of their color and form, there can be no pretense that they are as lively as they were when fresh. Fresh flowers are after all, alive, and dried ones are not. As a result, it is necessary to make a shift in perceptions about how the flowers can be arranged. It is, for example, very unlikely that a single dried flower in a slim vase will look good. It is much more likely to look sad and lacking in impact; its foliage will be crumpled and brittle, its stem will be sapless and the whole specimen will lack the unquestionable elegance of a live plant.

As a general rule, dried flowers are best arranged *en masse*, in dense and structured arrangements that exhibit the best of the colors and shapes of the preserved blooms. This requires quite a harvest in preparation for a design. For instance, a striking display of dried lavender may warrant fifty or a hundred stems of the flower rather than a gentle sprig or two. Similarly, the most successful dried-rose designs come in dozens of tightly packed blooms: Forget that one, perfect rose.

A rethink of containers is also involved. Clear glass vases that reflect elegant stems through clean water in fresh arrangements are largely unsuitable for dried flowers where rigid stalks would be seen through the glass, without the softening effect of water. There are, then, restrictions, but there is also the enormous benefit of using containers for the flowers that would not hold water for fresh flowers, providing new options for the dried flower arranger.

RIGHT *Dried seed pods take on a sculptural beauty that not apparent in the live plant, and that is a boon for dried flower and plant design.*

Bowl and vase arrangements

The most straightforward way of using dried or preserved flowers is to arrange them in bowls and vases as you might their live counterparts. The best varieties for this sort of treatment are flowers that can either be massed together to give volume and interest, or those which themselves consist of a mass of blooms or florets.

Hydrangeas

Hydrangeas were once a quintessential nineteenth-century English Victorian garden plant, seen lining the path of many a townhouse's front yard. In this context, they took on a serious air, with their static flower heads and subdued—even mournful—blues, purples, and pinks. The colors of the live flowers have a muted dusky appearance that makes them particularly appropriate for drying; the dried version is not very different from the live one, so the flower retains its integrity. The large heads, consisting of a mass of densely packed florets, also help their cause, since stems and foliage are already kept out of view by the plant itself. Just a few dried flower heads, with stems cut short, will support themselves in a small bowl, without the need for a complicated structure to back them up.

Dried hydrangeas are well suited to a traditional setting that harks back to their Victorian popularity. Small bowls placed on occasional tables around a living room, for example, look very pretty, taking on the appearance of potpourri. Blues and purples have a calm dignity that seems in keeping with genteel ideas of the past. The plant is coming back into fashion as a garden stalwart, and new varieties with pompom or flattened flower heads and a wider range of colors are particularly in vogue. Correspondingly, dried versions of the new flowers can grace contemporary interiors to good effect. Rounded, white (dried to something creamier) heads fulfill minimalist criteria, for example.

BELOW *Live hydrangeas have a soft, dusky appearance, often with their tiny petals in graduating shades of color. Mauves and blues have a particular solemnity.*

RIGHT *This small bowl is filled with a dome of dried hydrangea heads, their stems cut short. The purple-blue of the flowers contrasts well with the pale turquoise of the bowl.*

Bowl and vase arrangements

Flowers and foliage

Foliage plants tend to dry less successfully than flowering plants. There are some notable exceptions, such as eucalyptus, which keeps its shape and color well, but many delicate leaves wither to unrecognizable shapes and lose their intense greenness during the drying process. For dried flower artists, then, the word foliage encompasses a wide range of elements, including grasses and seed pods that will give the equivalent background to flowers in a preserved design. They offer neutral background shades of pale green and beige to counterbalance the colors of the flowers. A mixed group of flowers alone, without background, might otherwise look somewhat chaotic, and the beauty of the flowers and bands of color would be difficult to distinguish.

Inevitably, there is a different overall tone in dried flower arrangements, which can never quite have the vibrancy of living ones. The more muted shades of the flowers work well with the paler shades of the added "foliage," whereas brilliant greens would be domineering, rather than complementary. A different design eye needs to be developed, one that can provide combinations of colors from a more subdued palette.

BELOW A formal "posy" arrangement of pink and red dried rosebuds is displayed in a glass vase, but the unattractive stalks are cleverly hidden by crumpled red fabric in a shade halfway between that of the two rose varieties.

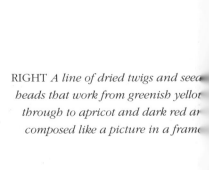

RIGHT A line of dried twigs and seed heads that work from greenish yellow through to apricot and dark red are composed like a picture in a frame.

Bowl and vase arrangements

Containers need to follow suit; very bright colors, of a different tonal quality to the dried flowers, or vividly patterned containers, will unbalance a design, and the whole will be unharmonious. The flowers must dominate an arrangement in order to look lively. Pots, pitchers, vases, and baskets made of untreated and unpainted natural materials are a boon for dried flowers, since they often share very similar tones and textures. A basket, after all, is made from dried plant stems or leaves, and therefore can't fail to have something in common with its contents. The tones of terracotta and stone are similarly natural and subdued, and often have an antique, weathered look that is also in keeping with dried flowers. You might be surprised to find how good dried arrangements look in metal containers, though they are almost exact opposites in terms of color and material. Dried lavender bundles in a metal stand have a strikingly cool, modernist feel.

ABOVE *Golden yellow and purple blooms are carefully massed in groups so their colors and shapes are clearly seen. The color of the seed head foliage is echoed in a silk fabric inside the vase.*

RIGHT *The potential problem of stems seen through glass is solved here by hiding them among pebbles and shells. The shape of the vase and choice of plants gives this arrangement a modern look.*

OPPOSITE *Hollow tubes of bamboo sunk into sand and pebbles are sympathetic oriental containers for spikey globe thistles.*

Dried roses

BELOW *The tall stems of wheat that give*
this design height and lightness are echoed
in the neatly clipped stalks of the basket
container. Together, they form a perfect
frame for the pink roses.

R oses dry superbly well, holding their just-opened bud shapes and
their colors (although it is hard to dry full-blown roses, which will
almost certainly shed their petals in the process). They also have a traditional feel similar to that of hydrangeas when they are used in simple vase
arrangements; the scent of dried roses is nostalgic, as though the romance
of past years is frozen in time. Dried roses massed together work well on
their own, in single color and type arrangements—white or red have a

LEFT *The colors of a verdigris metal dish are enhanced by the contrast of scarlet dried roses in a mound at its center.*

particularly powerful appeal. Roses also combine well with other dried flowers, perhaps providing the balance with their rounded shapes in a mixed vase with taller, slimmer flower varieties.

An antique appeal is, then, comparatively easy to achieve, but dried roses are also used in some up-to-the-minute designs. The regular, rounded shape of the flower heads means that a quantity of roses can be shaped into a sphere or dome very successfully. The round of each flower and the circular pattern of its individual petals complement the geometry of such designs and produce an interesting, graphic quality, especially if only one color of rose is used. As a result, roses are arranged in a regular pattern around spheres of florist's dry foam, which can then be hung from strings or balanced in the necks of bowls and vases. A half sphere of foam will produce a convincing treetop "topiary" of dried roses, attached at the top of sturdy branches and "planted" in a small pot.

ABOVE *A tiered effect in a willow basket lends an eye-catching geometry to this arrangement, which is achieved by trimming the stems to three different lengths and "planting" them upright.*

Dried roses

RIGHT *These cleverly sculpted and balanced flowerpots, each only about a foot high, create the illusion of miniature standard rose bushes.*

The stems of florist's roses are sturdy, even when they are dry, and will thus stand up completely straight in low containers, allowing yet more variations on a modern design theme. Their leaves are fairly robust, too, and generally appear more pleasing when dried than those of many other flowering plants. Garden roses can be similarly straight and strong, although other shrub and climbing varieties will have a more free-flowing habit that cannot be marshaled into such regularity.

Climbing roses can still be dried, as can those with multiple flower heads, miniature spray roses, and even wild dog roses. All need to be dried before they are fully open, and this is certainly much harder to time with single-petal varieties, which are more fragile. All in all, roses are a versatile element of a dried flower arranger's harvest.

LEFT *Masses of delicate, lacy dried sea lavender act as a mysterious foil for scarlet rosebuds. The red, white, and black of this design are very striking.*

BELOW *Small pink roses—in the subtlest of shades—nipped and dried in the bud, coordinate well with poppy seedheads of the same size and shape.*

Dried lavender

The Mediterranean herb lavender famously retains its soothing fragrance when dried, hence its popularity over the centuries as an ingredient of potpourri and as the content of sachets used to perfume stored linen and clothes. Lavender has been consistently in fashion since the Middle Ages. Recent, renewed interest in the medicinal uses of herbs has also revived lavender as a herb that induces rest and relaxation, and its essential oil is added to bathwater and sprinkled on bed pillows.

A versatile plant

Whereas many herbs give off perfume only from their leaves, and other plants only have scented flowers, all the elements of the lavender plant are strongly aromatic—stems, leaves, and flowers. As a result, even a small bunch of stems is powerful enough to perfume a room.

Lavender not only smells great, but it looks lovely, too. Varieties have flowers ranging from pale mauve through to deep violet-blue, and many retain their color well when dried. The plant is a hardy evergreen shrub that is easy to grow in the garden as a source for the cut herb. If a large amount is required, lavender can be grown as a hedging plant, particularly along a path where its scent can be fully appreciated. For contrasting colors, old English lavender (*Lavandula officinalis*), which has silver-gray leaves and pale, gray-blue flowers, could be grown with the deep purple 'Hidcote' variety, or 'Twickle Purple,' the stems of which can reach up to three feet in height.

BELOW This herb ring is made of lavender and hops woven and wired around a base. Its dark-blue and lime-green colors give it a fashionable look that would look fabulous against stone.

OPPOSITE A study of lavender hung up to dry makes clear the simple beauty of the stems and flower heads.

Dried lavender

ABOVE *A simple posy of lavender, tied with ordinary string, is still very pretty. A freshly cut bunch can be allowed to dry out gradually and decoratively.*

The stems of lavender are quite strong and supple, and can therefore be used in dried flower arrangements in a number of ways. They are robust enough to be pushed into dry florist's foam in formal designs. The lavender may be used as part of a mixed floral display, adding height, dark contrast, and spearlike shape to a design of more rounded flower varieties. Alternatively, lavender can be used alone in some quantity to make stunning dark-blue, fragrant topiary shapes of spheres or, for a contemporary look, cubes and other geometric figures.

Lavender stalks are flexible enough to bend around to be woven carefully into dried flower garlands, particularly those that incorporate other dried herbs and are intended to fragrance a room. Small posies of dried lavender can be placed in a guest bedroom, tied with satin ribbon, or incorporated as part of a table decoration—perhaps tied around the napkins, or slipped through the napkin ring. Lavender has so many uses that it is hard to imagine a dried-flower collection that does not include it near the top of the list.

Blue and white with larkspur

Larkspur retains its intense blue color after drying, and its tall stalks are resilient. The dried flowers look wonderful used in a great quantity on their own and are particularly suited to an arrangement in blue and white china—here, the container is a traditional tobacco jar with its lid removed. You could equally well use a blue and white bowl or even a piece of tableware, such as a vegetable dish, but make sure it has a large enough base to be well balanced and that it is big enough to work visually with the long stems of the larkspur.

1 Fill the bottom of the jar with crumpled newspaper, and add some weight if the arrangement threatens to be unstable. Wedge the florist's foam block into the jar. Start pushing the larkspur into the foam, lowest stems first and at right angles, to provide the basic structure.

2 Build around the skeleton shape, pushing the larkspur in evenly around the whole area of the florist's foam. The stems should all be of a similar length. Turn the jar as you work so you can view it in the round.

3 Continue until there is an even distribution of larkspur, with no gaps. If the flower heads look uneven, you can trim them with a pair of scissors to achieve a perfect rounded shape.

LEFT The finished tobacco jar display here has a wired satin ribbon arranged around the neck as insurance against a glimpse of florist's foam.

287

Grasses, twigs, & berries

Fall is harvest time for dried flower designers, as well as for farmers. A fantastic array of colors and forms is there in the natural world to be plundered—shiny red, yellow, or black berries; intricate sculptural pods; all manner of swaying grasses that have gone to seed; and wonderful, sinuous twigs and stems.

Fruits of field and forest

In order to acquire the elements that make really interesting and unusual arrangements, the dried plant enthusiast needs to develop something of a beachcomber mentality. What might at first appear to be boring broken twigs or rotting acorns that crunch underfoot, might, in fact, be the piece of nature that brings an otherwise conventional design to life. Gather whatever you find that is intrinsically attractive, take it home, and think about its decorative potential.

A fallen branch, for example, may have a bend or an angle that inspires a whole geometric design; wild pods shed their seeds to reveal patterns of cavities that have an inimitable geometry; and the fruits of trees—pine cones, bunches of sycamore "helicopters," sweet chestnuts—all have possibilities. Moss, tree bark, the tendrils of wild climbing plants, unharvested wheat, oats, and barley at the edges of fields, bright autumnal leaves—there is a wealth of material outside in the forests, on the waysides, on a country path, riches that are there for the keen eye to spot.

BELOW *A harvest festival display of wheat, barley, and safflowers, fresh pears, and a basket of colorful gourds.*

LEFT *The neutral shades of grasses and seed pods complement the pastel colors of dried garden flowers.*

ABOVE *Rose hips are tightly packed with seeds and are a hard, firm fruit. As a result, they dry without disintegrating and keep their bright, shiny exteriors.*

As we have seen, grasses, stems, and pods are the "foliage" plants of the dried checklist that form the structure and background of arrangements of dried flowers. Here they play a subsidiary role, but they can work equally well in their own right. In fact, nonflowering dried plants are fast becoming twenty-first-century stars. Fashions for interiors decorated with neutral colors, dependent on textures and shapes for their decorative appeal, have a natural affinity with such decorative plants. A vase with a few tall, straw-colored dried stalks with interestingly shaped seed pods, for example, looks much more appropriate and stylish in a minimalist loft than a bowl of more conventional dried flowers.

The beachcomber analogy is particularly apt if you consider the extent to which the seashore has invaded our homes, in the form of rows of eastern-inspired pebbles along window ledges, driftwood mirror frames, and glass vases filled with sea-shells. A decorative extension inland was inevitable, and dried plants have found their place in a modern context.

ABOVE *This graphic design of cinnamon, nutmeg, cut chili peppers, fungi, and bay leaves is designed to be viewed from above.*

LEFT *Cinnamon sticks and dried bay leaves are sculpted into candle holders and tied with raffia.*

Berries and fruits

Nature intends that its berries and fruits are eaten so the seeds they contain are dispersed. To attract the birds and other animals that will fulfill this task, the fruits of the plant must catch their attention with their bright colors and shiny, appetizing exteriors. Intense scarlet, orange, gold, yellow, and black lend berries an enormous decorative appeal. Many are easily found in the garden—rose hips, honeysuckle, viburnum, pyracantha, and ivy, for instance.

Some fruits, such as decorative hot peppers, hold their color well when dried whole, as do certain fungi, such as mushrooms. Pumpkins and gourds have a long life before they start to rot and decay, and the brilliant yellows, oranges, and greens of their skins can provide the centerpiece of arrangements incorporating less colorful dried ingredients, which lend an arrangement texture and shape. Other fruits can be specially cut and dried to retain color and pattern. Slices of apple or orange have wonderful textures and geometric pattern. Some unprepossessing vegetables also dry out decoratively: Whole garlic bulbs hold their shape and papery white exteriors, for example. Neither should nuts be ignored; those left over and past their prime could well be used to good effect.

OPPOSITE AND ABOVE *A garland uses moss, cones, fungi, and catkins as earthy contrast to bright pink heather; flax seeds make up a wreath with a textural appeal.*

293

Fruits of field and forest

ABOVE *An autumnal wall design includes a harvest of vegetables, including corn-on-the-cob and zucchini.*

RIGHT *A detail of the wall design shows the clever use of dried chili peppers to give dashes of accent color.*

OPPOSITE *Grasses, cereals, and poppy seed heads provide a complex palette of neutral color for brighter flowers and Chinese lanterns.*

Dried grasses and cereals are a boon to the modern dried plant arranger. Whereas ears of wheat are traditionally displayed in twisted, sheaflike bunches or in fanned sprays, contemporary designers have manipulated them to stand bolt upright, tightly bound and trimmed to the same height, to produce straight lines and geometric shapes. And some of the less sturdy grasses, such as hair grass or wall barley, are allowed to bend and curve in vases to form fluid dome shapes.

The future is rich for dried plant arrangements for the home. There is enormous scope for invention and imagination as more and more elements of the natural world are called into decorative play.

Celebrations

LEFT *Parcels of Chinese lanterns, candles in cutout paper bags, and bunches of cinnamon sticks hang from a line, held with clothespins and raffia, in a design that puts paper chains to shame.*

Many of the traditional festive dates of the calendar occur in the fall and winter months; at exactly the times when we would like to have a house full of fresh flowers, there are few in bloom outdoors. Although, of course, the florist will provide fresh out-of-season flowers all year round, dried flowers and plants are a rich alternative. Evergreens, berries, fruits, and seed pods, in particular, make fitting decorations in fall and winter, since they are true to the seasons in question.

Embellishing the house for a fall celebration, such as a Halloween party, for example, is the perfect opportunity to use the rich orange, copper, and red of the natural fall palette. Outside, the leaves on the trees are turning through colors, and they look wonderful inside, too. Central to most Halloween displays, after all, is a pumpkin of yellow fire as seen through a brilliant orange mask. An echo of fire and its associated colors can then be used throughout a scheme.

One of the most enchanting herbaceous garden perennials is *Physalis alkekengi*, commonly known as the Chinese lantern. It is a hardy plant that grows in all sorts of sites, sunny or shady, and in most soils, yet it looks almost too exotic to be so straightforward and easily available. Its

OPPOSITE *Orange ribbons to match exactly hold Chinese lantern seed heads and nigella seed heads around each napkin for a fall dinner party.*

297

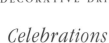

Celebrations

fruits are contained in bright orange, paper-thin, dangling lanterns that retain all their color and texture when they are cut and dried. Combined with the candlelight and pumpkin colors of an autumnal display, Chinese lanterns positively glow with complementary color.

Thanksgiving, Hanukkah, winter gatherings, and Christmas celebrations are usually characterized by a darker palette of red, green, and brown of plants that can be harvested in the final months of the year. Dried decorations at this time do not have to be predictable and limited in color, though, as the designs illustrated here clearly show.

BELOW *No one greeted by this vigorous table swag of flowers and fruit would expect to be anything less than well fed at the party it decorates. A substantial piece, it is secured to the underside of the table with nails to support its weight.*

The winter festivals are marked by a sense of abundance—typically in the form of lavish feasts—and the idea of excess can be carried through to the decorations. The wonderful, extravagant swag illustrated below is like something from a seventeenth-century Dutch still-life painting. All the fruits of the season are pulled together, and the swag complements the bowls of nuts and edible fruits on the table. On the right below, a classic-looking winter decoration is given an exotic edge by the inclusion of spicy bundles of cinnamon sticks and huge lotus seed heads, so the basket is far from ordinary. Add a ribbon of plaid as a nod to tradition.

BELOW *This basket is crammed with nuts, cones, seed heads—and pomanders of cloves that give it an exotic, spicy aroma. A restrained use of gold spray paint on some of the cones and the addition of gold ribbons lifts the colors of the basket without going over the top.*

Beachcomber wreath

The idea of this wreath is to make a decorative piece from what you might find during a walk on the beach, so different natural elements from those employed here could also be used—such as driftwood and twigs. It is important to include some pretty shells, so if you do not find enough, you could buy a bag of shells quite cheaply. The other ingredients are large dried thistle or artichoke heads, pieces of coral, and dried moss or lichen.

1 Use a wreath base, and bunch up pieces of dry sea lavender or other plants. Tie them with florist's wire, then attach them with small lengths of wire wrapped around the wreath.

2 Attach the thistles or artichoke heads and pieces of coral the same way, using loops of wire. Attach groups of shells, positioned to overlap, with a glue gun.

3 Glue on clusters of seaweed the same way to make a pleasing arrangement of color and texture. Fill gaps with glued-on moss or lichen. Finally, tie a large bow of rope or cord, and attach it with a loop of wire.

Index of plants for dried arrangements

Dried flower and plant arrangements need more planning and forethought than live designs—if an ingredient is missing, it can't be instantaneously snipped from the garden. The following comprehensive index of plants that are suitable for drying will provide a good checklist of varieties to plan for and to grow for drying. It also shows a few florist's blooms and, when you really need a few cheats, some convincing synthetic flowers and berries.

Index of dried flowers

The following pages index, first, flowering plants that are suitable for drying; second, foliage plants; and third, a mixture of plants and other elements of the natural world that are suitable for dried arrangements. If you are planning a garden patch of plants for cutting and drying, bear in mind a variety of shapes, heights, textures, and colors that will give as many decorative options as possible.

ABOVE *Hybrid tea roses, of the kind that are grown traditionally in small gardens, are available in a spectrum of colors. These yellow roses dry to a dark gold, seen here.*

LEFT AND RIGHT *African marigolds* (Tagetes erecta) *come in strong, dark orange and copper shades; goldenrod* (Solidago canadensis) *is a useful plant for height and texture.*

ABOVE *Bachelor's buttons* (Centaurea cyannus) *are cultivated for the yard in a number of different colors, such as this dark pink, which holds well when dry.*

ABOVE AND RIGHT *Carnations* (Dianthus sp.) *will dry quite well, but tend to lose some color; Helichrysum is nicknamed the everlasting flower, since it does just that, and is traditionally used in winter flower arrangements.*

BELOW *Clockwise: Achillea has wide, robust bracts that stay in good shape; lavender is the queen of dried herbs, treasured for its color and scent; poppy seed heads give shape and character to dried arrangements, acting in place of foliage.*

ABOVE *Miniature floribunda roses dry very successfully, easily holding the shape of their blooms and bracts.*

BELOW *From left to right: Hydrangea arborescens 'Annabelle' is a modern variety with pale green flowers that coordinate well with blues; the safflower (Carthamus tinctorius) is a popular flower that comes in a range of brilliant oranges, reds, and yellows; and blue bachelor's buttons dry a dark violet.*

ABOVE *Larkspur (Consolida ambigua) is a prime tall flower used in dry arrangements, and any of its flower heads that drop can be added to potpourri for color.*

Index of dried flowers

BELOW *Working from the top down, these parchment flowers are as follows: Rosebud; hydrangea; ornamental grass; peony, primula; iris; peony; poppy; wild rose; small rose; and cabbage rose.*

The flowers on this page are cheats—artificial flowers made from parchment—and they demonstrate here how similar they are to the genuine dried article. Do not necessarily abandon a planned design because you are missing one or two ingredients; these synthetic flowers will mix well with geniune dried flowers, tricking the eye into believing they are the real thing.

LEFT AND RIGHT *Back to the real, dried article, a wonderful dark red hydrangea,* Hydrangea macrophylla; *and small spray chrysanthemums that have dried dark gold.*

ABOVE *These safflowers have been picked while still in bud, so the flower heads appear like green burrs and the plant can be used as tall foliage.*

FROM LEFT *Clockwise: Small spray roses from a florist dry well, although care needs to be taken with their foliage; dudinea* (Dodonaea viscosa) *gives an opportunity for really bright red; and florist's standard roses, here a pleasing pinkish red.*

Index of dried flowers

LEFT AND BELOW Achillea ptarmica *'the Pearl' is one of a small number of flowers that stays creamy white when dry;* Alchemilla mollis, *so popular in live arrangements, loses its flower color a little when dry, but retains its cloudy softness.*

LEFT AND BELOW Eucalyptus *is perhaps most useful true foliag plant for drying; and lies-bleeding (*Amaran sp.*) darkens, but keep. height and texture.*

ABOVE *The soft, tufty thistle heads of* Centaurea macrocephala *provide good tall shape and texture to larger dried arrangements.*

ABOVE *This lavender is the variety 'Hidcote,' a dark, violet blue that also gives height and contrasts well with all shades of yellow and gold.*

LEFT AND ABOVE *The colorful dropped petals of dried flowers can be mixed together to make bright and fragrant potpourri; these berries are plastic, but look real enough to be used to add color to dried arrangements.*

LEFT AND RIGHT *A real favorite, for its spiky appearance, spherical shapes, and dark blue-gray color is the globe thistle (*Echinops ritro*); large, lime-green hydrangea heads contrast well in shape and color with the echinops.*

ABOVE *Sea lavender (*Goniolimon tartaricum*) has insignificant flowers but a tangle of slender stems, which give background and texture and lightness of color.*

LEFT TO RIGHT *These flowers and foliage would combine well in a stylish dried design: a large pink peony; the decorative pods of Thalictrum; a large-leafed eucalyptus; and the seed pods of the money plant (*Lunaria *sp.*).

Index of dried elements

ABOVE *Small terracotta flowerpots can become part of a dried flower design; they can even be wired onto wreaths to good effect.*

ABOVE LEFT AND RIGHT
Fungi are worth experimenting with, as some common varieties dry well and are an unusual decorative component for dried designs.

CENTER AND ABOVE *Many evergreen cones dry well: These small larch cones are rich tawny brown; lotus seed heads are widely available to buy and are prized for the geometric pattern of their seed cavities; farmers' wheat grows tall, straight, and regular, the epitome of fall.*

FROM LEFT *Clockwise: Moss—in all its varieties—is invaluable to fill corners, provide a green backdrop, and cover the structures of wreaths or florist's foam; dried apple slices take on a decorative role; small oranges, sliced to make a pattern and aid drying, look very pretty and combine well with orange and red helichrysum heads.*

ABOVE *Finally, an indispensable dried plant— strands of the raffia leaf. This stalwart is the ideal and complementary dried element to tie around dried arrangements and posies.*

RIGHT AND FAR RIGHT *Globe artichokes dry to a pale, gentle color, and have a marvelous leaf structure. Smooth, shiny birch twigs are a favorite with modern dried plant designers.*

311

Index

Index of plant names

General Index

Acknowledgements

I have had a spectacular array of flower arrangements to choose from when compiling this book, and I am very grateful to the inspirational floral artists whose work is illustrated.

Many thanks to Kate Kirby at Collins & Brown for her spirited and sustained commissioning of the book; to Jane Ellis for her calm masterminding of the project; and to the editorial and design team at Axis. At home, my thanks go to wonderful Oli.

Photograph credits

Elizabeth Whiting & Associates pp 7, 10–11, 70–1, 80–1, 164–5, 168–9, 275, 288–9, 302–3; **The Garden Picture Library** pp 18, 58–9; **The Interior Archive Ltd** pp 136–7; **Adobe Interiors Photography & Library** pp 172–3.
All other photographs Collins & Brown Ltd.